To

FREDERICK LEWIS GAY, A.B.

WHOSE VALUABLE COLLECTION OF BYLES MANUSCRIPTS
AND PORTRAITS HAS MUCH ENRICHED MY KNOWL-
EDGE OF MATHER BYLES, AND TO WHOM I
AM OTHERWISE INDEBTED FOR HELP
IN MY WORK, WITH SINCERE
REGARD I DEDICATE
THIS BOOK

THE AUTHOR

67261

CONTENTS

ILLUSTRATIONS

THE FAMOUS MATHER BYLES

CHAPTER I

THE FAMOUS MATHER BYLES

FROM the shadows of pre-Revolutionary Boston no single figure emerges in whom sympathetic historians find a greater variety of interest than in the Tory preacher, poet, and humourist, who appears commonly in our annals as the "famous" or "celebrated" Doctor Mather Byles. In days when religious discussion was acrid and local political feeling ran high and vituperation of opponents was often incredibly bitter, Mather Byles's witticisms kept Boston laughing immoderately for at least a generation, and no doubt tended not a little to the softening of asperities in the popular life, and it is naturally as one of New England's earliest humourists that Byles has been most conspicuously mentioned in periodicals and books. But the man has an interest far wider than that of a "punning divine," the age through which he lived was the most dramatic in our annals and his own life lacks no single element that gives the time picturesqueness, while the aloofness from politics he persistently maintained puts him out of the category of those who in the fierce Revolutionary struggle actively helped or hindered the great cause to which the majority of his fellow townsmen gave their ardent support.

That no one has hitherto taken the trouble to write the life of Mather Byles is not strange. He was a grandson of Increase and a nephew of Cotton Mather, and his striking personality, his keen intellectual gifts, and his prolific writings give him a worthy place beside those remarkable men, but he lived through the Revolution and in that momentous conflict gave countenance to the losing side, and among the Congregational ministers of New England, as with the Patriots generally, he stood for the rest of his life, and his name continued to stand when he was dead, as a synonym for disloyalty and treachery of the basest kind. Moreover, at the evacuation of Boston his only living son, Mather Byles, Junior, went to Halifax with Howe's fleet, and in the Anglican church of St. Paul in that town, and in Trinity Church, St. John, New Brunswick, later, pursued the ministry which he had previously exercised at Christ Church, Boston, and when he died, all his descendants were living, as most of them have since lived, under the British flag.

Mather Byles has lately been brought before us picturesquely, and probably in a rather truthful way, in that charming imaginative brochure, that has had wide

reading, "Earl Percy's Dinner Table."
In that book, we find him during the
siege of Boston, among British officers in
scarlet tunics and gold lace, or in the blue
uniforms of His Majesty's Royal Navy,
and rich gentlemen merchants of the town
in silk and brocade, in velvet and lace, —
Lieutenant-Colonel John Gunning, Francis
Lord Rawdon; Lord Holland's son, Hon.
Henry Edward Fox, Captain Evelyn of the
King's Own, the young Cuthbert Colling-
wood, Major John Pitcairn, Colonel Isaac
Royal, and Roger Sheaffe — sipping his
port, and throwing the company into fits
of laughter by his witty sallies on "the
holy hypocrisy which is ruining the province," or on much less important personal
themes.   But "Earl Percy's Dinner Table"
is only the latest writing in which Doctor
Byles figures, no faithful chronicler of Revolutionary Boston but exploits his "persistent Toryism," or his "irrepressible wit,"
and no conscientious reviewer of early New

England literature but has something to say about the poetry and the published discourses of this brilliant descendant of the famous Mathers, and enthusiastic disciple of the poet Pope.

For more than forty years Doctor Byles was the faithful pastor of Boston's Hollis Street Congregational Church, and his striking gifts as a preacher, and the close relationship he bore to the Mathers and Cottons, make him an important figure in New England ecclesiastical annals. But he was besides a literary man of much ability, and reviewers of early New England prose and poetry, while not always enthusiastic in praise of his literary productions, have never failed to take respectful notice of his work. In the social life of Boston, moreover, Byles occupied a highly important place, and the marked preference he uniformly showed for persons of high official and social rank quite evidently created against him in the minds of his more democratic brethren of the Massachusetts clergy, a strong antagonism, that greatly increased their bitterness against him when he finally gave the weight of his influence against the popular cause in the Revolution. Doctor Byles married twice and by both marriages allied himself with influential families among the ruling class, and in his aristocratic sympathies, as in his persistent loyalty to England, his family, as was natural, deeply shared. As we have previously said, a conspicuous refugee within the British lines and later resident in Halifax, Nova Scotia, whither like most of the royalists of Boston, in March, 1776, he fled with General Howe, was his only living son, who for several years previous to the breaking out of the Revolution had been the Rector of Christ Church, in the north end of his native town.

That like the rest of the Tories in the Revolution Doctor Byles was sentenced to banishment our biography will presently show, but although formally proceeded against by the authorities as a person inimical to the welfare of the state, on account of his advanced age it may be, or perhaps from some lingering feeling that the sacredness of his office as a minister of the ruling faith of New England should exempt him from the severest treatment accorded political offenders, he was not sent out of the Colony, but was suffered to remain, a despised and lonely figure however, in Boston, to the end of his days. Of his last remaining descendants in Boston, his two unmarried daughters, the Misses Mary and Catherine Byles, as of their brother Doctor Mather Byles, Junior, before this book ends we shall have something to say. These ladies survived their father and lived on till about the middle of the nineteenth century in the old house in Tremont Street which their father had purchased in 1741, the most picturesque figures in Boston, cherishing fondly the recollections of the past, hating the Republic whose birth extreme ill-fortune had compelled them to see ushered in, and guarding sacredly their household treasures and precious heirlooms for the descendants of their brother, who lived under England's rule.

Of the actual forms and faces of many ancient worthies of New England we are often able to gain only the vaguest impression, in the cases of some, however, we are left in no possible doubt. Of Doctor Byles's friend Doctor William Walter, Rector of Trinity Church, Boston, we have the minute information that he was a handsome man, tall and well proportioned, with a serene countenance, indicating a serene temper, and that in the street he commonly wore an ample blue cloak over his cassock or long frock coat, a full-bottomed wig, dressed and powdered, knee breeches of fine black cloth, black silk stockings, and "square quartered"

shoes with silver buckles, his head covered
with an impressive three-cornered or cocked
hat. Concerning Doctor Byles's appearance tradition has been almost as explicit,
he was rather large, rather tall, rather fine
looking, altogether of commanding presence, and both in and out of the pulpit
he had a pleasing manner and voice.[1] How
he commonly dressed we are nowhere
plainly told, except that his wig was ample,
as the fashion dictated, that he wore a
cassock or long, close-fitting coat, probably
with a single row of buttons from the
waist to the neck, that the three-cornered
hat was also his head covering, and that
he usually carried a heavy cane. When
he was summoned to appear before the
members of his church for trial he is
described as having appeared in full flowing robes, of course with bands, but since
we do not feel certain regarding the time
when gowns came to be worn by New
England Congregational ministers in the

pulpit we do not feel quite sure of the accuracy of this account.

We are fortunate in having three admirable portraits of Doctor Byles, and these, taken at different times in his career, introduce us very familiarly to his face. The first of these portraits, like the well-known portrait of Cotton Mather that greets us in so many publications, was painted by Pelham, evidently almost immediately after Doctor Byles began his ministry, the other two were painted by Copley, one it is believed in 1768, the other in 1774, the same year in the early summer of which this great painter left Boston finally for Europe. In all three of these portraits Doctor Byles is represented in some sort of classical drapery, it is possible, indeed, an ordinary pulpit gown, the gown in Pelham's portrait, however, being painted a rich red. In all, his wig is full and curling, and in the latter two his face shows the strong characteristics we have become so familiar with in him as we have studied his life. Pelham's portrait sacrifices strength to attractiveness in the subject, Copley's, one painted when Doctor Byles was about sixty-one, the other when he was about sixty-seven, show him an accomplished looking, elderly man, with strong sense of superiority, keen intelligence, great nervous energy, a high-bred Roman nose, eyes that might easily sparkle with enlivening humour or gleam with fierce sarcasm, and a firm, decided mouth, from which might come the most kindly encouragements or the most scathing and bitter rebukes. A commanding personality, in which high principle predominated, but where serious outlook on life was frequently tempered with an almost riotous sense of humour, and lofty appreciation with dislike and contempt — this is the character of Doctor Byles that the fine portraits of him by Copley present to our minds.

Of these three distinguished portraits of Mather Byles the earliest one, that by Pelham, and the first of the two Copleys, are owned by Mr. Frederick Lewis Gay of Brookline, Massachusetts, the second Copley is still in the possession of Doctor Byles's descendants, its present owner being William Bruce Almon, Esq., M.D., of Halifax, Nova Scotia. This Copley portrait of Doctor Almon's, with the owner's kind permission we are able to present as the frontispiece of our book.

CHAPTER II

BIRTH, EDUCATION, JOURNALISTIC WRITINGS

In the last decade of the seventeenth century, when Boston was a little town of about ten thousand inhabitants, its square mile of area coextensive with the peninsula on which it was built, the "Neck," about two hundred feet wide at Dover Street, uniting the peninsula with the neighbour town of Roxbury, there came into the North End of Boston, from Winchester, Hants, England, a respectable saddler named Josias Byles. Until after the Revolution, well on into the nineteenth century in fact, the north part of Boston, including Dock Square and Hanover Street, and the extreme North End, about Copp's Hill, a region peopled now almost entirely

13

by Italians, was the home of a large number of the most active and prosperous, and indeed influential, people of the town. In 1711, a little later than the time of Josias Byles's arrival, the Honourable William Clark bought land on what is now North Square, and built a handsome house there, his friend Thomas Hutchinson, father of the last royal governor, building one near that was evidently meant to outshine his in magnificence.

Facing North Square stood the Old North or Second Church, the meetinghouse of the religious society whose affairs were ruled, and for the most part ruled wisely, for over seventy years, by ministers of the historic Mather family, the Reverend Doctor Increase Mather, his son the illustrious Cotton Mather, and for a while, until serious disaffection arose in the society and he moved away with a portion of his people and founded a new society, the Rev. Doctor Samuel Mather, Cotton

REVEREND INCREASE MATHER
From the original painting by Vanderspriet, 1688

Mather's much less important son.[2]   When
Josias Byles came to Boston, Doctor Increase Mather was well along in his ministry of the Old North Church,[3] and his
son Cotton was colleague with him, the
older minister living on North Street, the
younger probably then as later living on
Hanover Street, not far from the church.
Josias Byles may have come to Boston
late in 1693 or early in 1694, for he had
a young child buried in the Granary
Burying Ground in April of the latter
year, and he undoubtedly settled at once
in the North End.   When he came his
family consisted of his wife Sarah and
three or four young children, and after
he had lived two or three years in Boston,
on the 11th of October, 1696, he connected himself formally with Doctor Increase Mather's church.   In Boston the
Byleses had at least four children born and
soon after the birth of her youngest child
Mrs Byles died.   Within a year after her

death, on the 6th of October, 1703, a widower and with several young children, a saddler and in not remarkably good circumstances, Josias Byles married, rather ambitiously we should suppose, his pastor Rev. Increase Mather's second daughter, Elizabeth, widow of William Greenough, a lady of between thirty-seven and thirty-eight years old, Mr. Byles being then about forty-seven.

After his second marriage and probably before, Josias Byles lived, so tradition says, in what became in 1821 Tileston Street, a street first formally laid out about 1806, which runs from near the lower end of Hanover Street to Salem Street and is the northern boundary of the block of which North Bennet Street is the southern.   In less than five years, however, after his second marriage, to the last pursuing the saddler's trade, Mr. Byles suddenly died, but from these less than five years dates the Byles family's chief subsequent importance in Boston. The precise event in which the family's conspicuousness takes its rise is the birth on the 15th of March, 1707, a little less than a year before the father died, of a son whose coming into the world united indissolubly the comparatively unknown Byles family with the great ecclesiastical houses of Mather and Cotton. To this son, who may have appeared rather unexpectedly, for so far as we know Elizabeth Byles had never borne a child before, in recognition of his distinguished ancestry on his mother's side the name Mather was promptly, most appropriately given.

That Josias Byles should have married, as far as we can tell without protest on the part of its members, into the notable Mather family, shows conclusively that the late-emigrating Englishman was regarded as a man of much worth, and his general good standing is further declared by Chief-Justice Sewall's respectful men-

c

tion of him in his famous Diary, where,
under date of "Midweek, March 17,
1707/8," he records: "my Country-man,
M.ʳ Josiah Byles dyed very suddenly."
Soon after he writes: "Reginald Odell
dies suddenly. Heard of it at M.ʳ Byles
Funeral." But it is quite as evident that
the saddlery in Tileston Street had not
yielded its proprietor very large profits,
for although when Josias Byles died he
left a gentlemanly will, in which he bade
his children by his first wife behave with
dutiful respect towards their stepmother,
and charged his eldest son Josias, Jr., to
give his stepmother all the help he could
in carrying on the saddler's trade if she
wished to continue it, he left very little
property for his widow and her child or
indeed any of his family, and M.ʳˢ Byles
soon had to be helped by her kind brother
Cotton. In his journal, on the 23d of
December, 1711, Cotton Mather writes:
"I have a Sister, a Widow, in some Wants

and Straits. I will dispense Releefs unto
her particularly in regard of her Habit."
And again, January 17, 1714: "I have a
Widow-sister, who greatly needs to be
putt into a Way of subsisting herself,
and to be animated unto the use of her
own vigorous Endeavours for that Purpose." Still again, January 31, 1714: "I
must proceed with further Contrivances
and Assistances, that my Widow-sister
may be well provided for."

When the widow Byles's son Mather
was a little over seventeen, his grandfather,
Increase Mather died, and in this learned,
methodical minister's will, which he had
written about five years before his death,
we find the aged testator saying: "What
I give to my daughter Elizabeth I desire
may (if his mother can) be improved
towards ye education of her only son (my
grandson Mather Byles) in Learning, because he is a child whom God has blessed
with a strong memory & ready capacity

& aptness to learn. I leave it as my dying Request to his uncle my son Cotton Mather, to take care of ye education of y^t child as of his owne. If he shall obtain subscriptions for his education for ye ministry (as he knows I have done for more fatherless children y^n one) I am persuaded y^t his owne children will not fare ye worse for his being a father to a fatherless child. To prevent his being Chargable as much as I can I give him my wearing apparel excepting my chamber cloak wch I give to my executor.

"If ye Lord shall take away Mather Byles by death before he is of full age (or if he shall not be employed in ye work of ye ministry it is my mind & will y^t then ye Books bequeathed to him shall be given to such other of my grand children as shall be preachers of ye Gospel of Christ according as my executors shall dispose." A fourth part of his library the testator bequeaths to his fatherless grandson Mather

Byles, in case Byles shall be "educated for & employed in ye work of ye ministry," which he much desires and prays for, and he mentions certain books he wishes him to have, leaving others, however, to be chosen by his executors.

That Cotton Mather already felt the proper interest in his nephew is shown by an entry in his diary of the 15th of April, 1711, in which he says feelingly : "I must be much of a Father to the fatherless child of my Sister Biles.   One thing I particularly now propose ; that I will give him the little Book of 'Good Lessons for Children,' and give him a Peece of Money for every one of the Lessons that he learns without a Book." [4]   Later, he several times speaks with the greatest solicitude of his nephew's poor physical condition.   The boy is said to have been put to school at the North Latin School in Bennet Street, near his home, and at this institution he probably got his preparation for college.   In 1721

Byles entered, as a matter of course, the college at Cambridge, of which his grandfather Increase had been president for sixteen years, where his uncle Cotton had graduated in 1678, his uncle Nathaniel in 1685, and his uncle Samuel in 1690, and of which every one of his ministerial relatives who had lived in and near Boston, by virtue of his clerical office had been an overseer.[5] But towards the end of his college course his health became extremely poor and it was feared he was going to die of consumption. March 18, 1724, his uncle Cotton writes: "My poor Nephew, under Languishments, what shall be done for him?" April 1st, 1724, he writes: "The dangerous condition of my Nephew M. B. in regard of his Entring into a Consumption requires me to do all I can for him; especially to prepare him for what he may be coming to." April 22d he writes: "My Kinsman, M. B., being fallen, I doubt, into a Consumption, I must with all possible

Cottonus Matherus

S. Theologiæ Doctor Regiæ Societatis Londinensis Socius,
et Ecclesia apud Bostonum Nov-Anglorum nuper Præpositus.

Ætatis Suæ LXV, MDCCXVII.

Goodness and Concern sett myself to do all
that I can find proper to be done for a
Nephew in such circumstances." In the
autumn of this year Byles's life was evidently despaired of, for on the 28th of October Cotton Mather writes: "Lord what
shall I do, for my two Nephews, whose Life
drawes near to the Grave?" In spite of his
uncle's fears, however, Byles fully recovered,
and in 1725, when a little over eighteen,
left college with his bachelor's degree.[6]

The Harvard class of which Mather
Byles was the thirteenth member in social
rank, a dozen of the sons of public officials
and others coming before him, at graduation numbered forty-five, but though earlier
classes had had a large proportion of
ministers among their members, this class
had besides Byles, so far as we can dis-
cover, only two who adopted a ministerial
career.[7] Whether Byles himself for a time
after graduation wavered in his choice of
a profession we do not know, nor have we

learned what if any subsequent training he took for the ministry, but it was 1729 before he seems to have been thought of for a parish, and it was not until late in 1733 that he was ordained.[8] It would be exceedingly interesting to know if we could precisely what the relations were between Byles and his fellow students and the tutors of the college during the four years they spent together at Harvard, but on this point likewise we have little light. That Byles gave special attention to literature, especially poetry, is clearly the case but from his general intelligence and love of learning there is no reason to doubt that he gave creditable care to the routine studies of his Freshman, Sophomore, Junior Sophister, and Senior Sophister years. In October, 1723, a committee of visitation, of which Judge Sewall was chairman, made a curious report on the moral condition of the Harvard student body, in which they say: "Although there is a

considerable number of virtuous and studious youth in the college, yet there has
been a practice of several immoralities;
particularly stealing, lying, swearing, idle-
ness, picking of locks, and too frequent use
of strong drink; which immoralities, it is
feared, still continue in the college, notwithstanding the faithful endeavours of the rulers
of the House to suppress them."   Of the two
contrasted groups mentioned in this fierce
arraignment of the students of Harvard in
1723 we judge that Mather Byles and his
intimate friends stood among the "virtuous
and studious youth," rather than among the
swearing and lying young gentlemen who
picked locks and were too frequently given
to the use of strong drink, but we should
also like much to know whether the anger
of the whole student body and of Byles
among the rest was not fiercely aroused
by such a defamatory report of the college
as had been officially given by Sewall and
his censorious band.

In Doctor Byles's Freshman year in college appeared his first literary production in print. The *New England Courant*, the third newspaper to be published in Boston, made its earliest appearance on Monday, August 7, 1721, its owner, editor, and printer being James Franklin, Benjamin Franklin's older brother. The journalistic career of James Franklin was a somewhat turbulent one, for the spirit of its editor was distinctly aggressive, and in his newspaper "the government of the province and its principal agents, the clergy, and various individuals, were attacked by the editor and his correspondents, without much regard to public or personal character." [9] In 1721 and 1722 an engrossing subject of discussion in Boston was the value of inoculation for smallpox, the strongest champions of vaccination being the venerable Increase and his son Cotton Mather and its most vigorous and unsparing opponent the editor of the

New England Courant. In favour of inoculation, Increase Mather published a
pamphlet, entitled "Several Reasons, proving that Inoculating or Transplanting the
Small-Pox is a lawful Practice, and that
it has been blessed by God for the saving of many a Life," whereupon, and for
their general advocacy of vaccination, the
Courant lampooned both Mathers unmerci-
fully, the *Boston Gazette*, on the other hand,
taking their part and exalting the practice
highly.   In the course of the controversy,
in which personalities were indulged in to
a degree which even in these days of newspaper license seems almost impossible,
Doctor Mather sent his grandson Mather
Byles to Franklin with a manuscript article
giving an account of the success of inoculation in London, which Byles told the jour-
nalist he himself had copied from the *London
Mercury.* Franklin published the article,
but later declared in his paper that the
transcriber had changed it, so that it was

quite different from the original article in
the *Mercury*. Charging Byles, whom he
calls "our young spark," with deliberate
falsehood in reference to the article, he also
takes occasion to say that any measure
whatever advocated by ministers was sure
to be from the devil, and at least implies
that both Increase and Cotton Mather
had given currency to malicious state-
ments concerning the conduct of his paper.
In a letter to Franklin, which this editor
prints in his journal of January 29 to
February 5, 1722, Doctor Increase Mather
says:

"M: Franklin, I had Thoughts of taking
your Courant (upon Tryal) for a Quarter
of a Year, but I shall not now. In one of
your Courants you have said that *if the
Ministers of God are for a Thing* it is a
Sign it is from the Devil, and have dealt
very falsly about the *London Mercury*. For
these and other Reasons, I shall No More
be concerned with You." The malice of

the Mathers against his paper, so Franklin asserts, had expressed itself definitely in the slanderous charges that the *Courant* was "carried on by a Hell-Fire Club, with a Non-Juror at the head of them," this club being patterned after a conspicuous anti-religious club of men and women in London, bearing the name just given, whose blasphemies, as people regarded them, were notorious. In defending his paper against the charges of the Mathers and some other attacks of enemies of the journal, Franklin says: "These, with many other Endeavours, proceeding from an arbitrary and Selfish temper, have been attended with their hearty Curses on the *Courant* and its Publisher; but all to no purpose; for, (as a Connecticut trader once said of his onions) *The more they are cursed, the more they grow.* Notwithstanding which, a young scribbling Collegian, who has just Learning enough to make a Fool of himself, has taken it in his Head *to put a Stop to this Wickedness,* (as he calls it) by a Letter in the last Week's Gazette. Poor Boy ! When your Letter comes to be *seen in* other Countries, (under the Umbrage of Authority) *what* indeed *will they think* of New-England ! They will certainly conclude, *There is bloody fishing* for nonsense at Cambridge, and *sad work at the Colledge.* The young Wretch, when he calls those who wrote the several Pieces in the Courant the Hell-Fire Club of Boston, and finds a Godfather for them, (which, by the way, is a Hellish Mockery of the Ordinance of Baptism, as administered by the Church of England,) and tells us, *That all* the Supporters of the paper will be looked upon as Destroyers of the Religion of the Country, and Enemies to the faithful Ministers of it, little thinks what a cruel Reflection he throws on his Reverend Grandfather, who was then, and for some time before, a Subscriber for the Paper."

Byles's "letter in last week's Gazette" to which Franklin refers with such contempt will be found in the *Gazette* of January 15, 1722. It reads as follows:

"CAMBRIDGE, January 11, 1721 [old style]
"M.ʳ MUSGRAVE,

"When I read the Crimes laid to your Charge in the Scandalous *Courant* last Monday I was in some danger of entertaining a hard Character of you; but when I read on a little further, the danger was over. Finding the Wretches Charge you as imposing on the Publick when you inserted these words from the London Mercury, September 16, *Great Numbers in this City, and Suburbs are under the Inoculation of the Small Pox:* Every one said That if these Words were indeed there, the Publishers of this Impious and Abominable Courant, must be the most Audacious and Brazen-fac'd Liars in the World; not a Word is to be believed that shall be uttered by Fellows of such matchless and uncommon Impudence. Accordingly we examined the Mercury, and found the words every Syllable of them there. So we all concluded that you might be an honest Man, till better Men than they can prove an ill thing upon you.

"Every one sees that the main intention of this Vile Courant, is to Vilify and Abuse the best Men we have, and especially the Principal Ministers of Religion in the Country. And tho' they have been so left of God, and of Sense, as to tell People in Print, that they live in a Wickedness, which no country besides, whether Christian, Turkish, or Pagan, was ever known to be guilty of; yet they go on in it; and in this last Courant they taught the People, *That if the Ministers do approve, advise a thing, 'tis a Sign that it is of the Devil.* You see Sir, that you have Company of which you need not be ashamed.

"If such an horrid Paper, called the *New England Courant*, should be seen in other Countries, what would they think of New-England ! If you call this Crew, the *Hell-Fire Club of Boston*, your Friend *Campbell* will stand God-father for it; having in one of his News Papers formerly assign'd this proper Name for them. And all the sober People in the Country will say, They deserve it. . . . Be sure, all the Supporters of this Paper will be justly looked upon, as the Supporters of a *Weekly Libel* written on purpose to destroy the Religion of the Country, and as Enemies to the faithful Ministers of it. And if this Hell-Fire Paper be still carried on, you shall have a List of their Names, that all the Sober People in the Country may know who they are. I am not my self a Minister, nor have I advised with any such for this Letter; nor did I ever yet publish any thing. But there is a Number of us, who resolve, that if this wicked-

D

ness be not stop'd, we will pluck up our
Courage, and see what we can do in our
way to stop it.[10]   "I am

"Sir, Your Servant."

[The Signature not given.]

When we come to discuss Mather Byles
as a poet we shall see that he himself
affirms that in college he wrote a considerable number of poems, but whether the
letter he wrote to the *Gazette* during the inoculation controversy was his only as well as
his first contribution to journalism while he
was an undergraduate we cannot now tell.
In March, 1727, however, when he had been
almost two years out of college, he connected
himself as an editorial writer and contribu-
tor of articles in prose and poetry on important events of the day, with a newly starting
modest newspaper called the *New-England
Weekly Journal*.[11] The paper lasted until
1741, when it was incorporated with the
Boston Gazette, and in its early years, at

least, Byles contributed to it a good many
conspicuous prose articles and such poems
as that on the death of King George I
and the accession of George II, his flattering welcome to Governor Burnet, his "Conflagration," and his "Verses written in
Milton's Paradise Lost." The signature
to his prose articles, when they are signed,
is one of the letters C E L O I Z A.

Precisely how intimate Byles was with
his uncle Cotton Mather during the years
he spent in Cambridge and until Mather
died, in 1728, we should much like to
know, but we cannot help believing that
Mather's influence was strong with him,
and that in the intercourse he had with
this remarkable man Mather stimulated
Byles's intellectual activity, while he gave
his cordial approval to his nephew's connexion with the Weekly Journal. Whether
Mather, however, had anything directly
to do with Byles's training in theology or
homiletics, or whether before Mather died

it was even decided that Byles should enter the ministry we have seen no record whatever to show.   In the *Weekly Journal* of February nineteenth, 1728, appeared a laudatory obituary of Cotton Mather, which we believe bears strong internal evidence of having been composed by Mather Byles.   It reads in part as follows: "Last Tuesday in the forenoon between 8 and 9 o'clock died here the very Reverend Cotton Mather, Doctor in Divinity of Glasgo and Fellow of the Royal Society in London, Senior Pastor of the Old North Church in Boston, and an overseer of Harvard College; by whose Death persons of all ranks are in Concern and Sorrow. He was perhaps the principal ornament of this Country, and the greatest scholar that was ever bred in it."   The notice then goes on to tell of Mather's extensive charity, entertaining wit, singular goodness of temper, and the Divine Composure and joy with which he finished his Career.[12]

CHAPTER III

ORDINATION AND FIRST MARRIAGE

IN 1729 Mather Byles evidently felt himself ready for ordination, for in Clapp's "Ancient Proprietors of Jones Hill, Dorchester" we find the statement, no doubt taken from the Dorchester church records, that in that year, of three candidates considered for the position of colleague to the aged Dorchester pastor, Rev. John Danforth, Mr. Byles was one. The person chosen, however, was the Rev. Jonathan Bowman, and for some reason Mr. Byles's ordination, as we have said, did not take place until December 20, 1733, more than eight years after his graduation from college. Up to 1732 the Congregational churches of Boston numbered seven, the First Church organized in 1630; the Second

or Old North, in 1650; the Old South in
1669; the "Manifesto Church," later the
Church meeting in Brattle Square, in
1699; the New North, whose meeting-
house was on Hanover Street, in 1714;
the church whose meeting-house was on
Church Green, in 1719; and the Federal
Street Church (which began as a Pres-
byterian Church but became Congregational), in 1727. In January, 1730, the
Honourable Jonathan Belcher, who like
his father, M[r] Andrew Belcher, had become what Boston historians euphemis-
tically term a "very opulent merchant,"
and consequently a person of high importance in the commercial town, by adroit
political management while in England
had been able to get the appointment of
Governor of Massachusetts, and the Honourable William Tailer had been restored
to the lieutenant-governorship, which he
had held some time before. By this time
in the south suburb of the town, bordering

on the Neck, and especially along Orange
(Washington) Street, a good many houses
had been built, one of which, near the
junction of Hollis and Orange Streets, was
Governor Belcher's own country house.
From his father, Andrew Belcher, the Governor had inherited in this region a considerable quantity of land, which he probably
wanted to sell, and naturally he was
anxious to give people every inducement
he could to settle here. The Boston
churches we have enumerated were then
all located either in the North End of the
town or near the centre of the peninsula,
and Belcher among others determined to
erect a church in Hollis Street. Accordingly
this opulent merchant, then and for nine
years longer the chief official of the province,[13] gave a deed of a building lot for a
meeting house; on the 14th of November,
1732, a new religious society was organized,
and on the 20th of December, 1733, Mather
Byles was ordained pastor of the church.

Of the beginning of this church the author of the History of the Old South Church says: "The South Church took much interest in the gathering of Hollis Street Church, which was formed November 14. Governor Belcher gave the land on which the meeting house had been built; and Doctor Sewall drew up the form of covenant. Mather Byles, grandson of Increase Mather, was ordained as its first minister, December 20." "This day [November 14, 1732]," says the Rev. Joseph Sewall, "was kept as a Day of Prayer by the New Society at the South. Mᵣ Checkly began, then Mr. Cooper prayed. Doctor Colman preach'd from 2 Cor. 8:5. Then Mr. Webb prayd. Thirteen of the Brethren entred into Covenant, forming a distinct Church. I read the Covenant to them and then Prayd." Under date of December 20th, Mr. Sewall says: "Mᵣ Byles was ordain'd to the New Church. Mᵣ Prince

His Excellency. JONATHAN BELCHER Esq.
Captain General & Governor in Chief of His Majesty's Provinces of
Massachuset's Bay & New Hampshire in NEW ENGLAND and
Vice Admiral of the Same.

began with Pray'r. Mr. Byles preach'd
from 2 Timothy 3 : 17. Then Mr. Walter
pray'd. I gave the Charge, and D.ʳ Colman the right hand of Fellowship." [14]

From the time of his settlement over
the Hollis Street Church, as indeed most
likely before, Mr. Byles was evidently on
terms of the closest friendship with Governor Belcher, though whether the governor
at any time of year commonly attended
service at the new church, having his
pew in the Old South, where ever since its
removal from Cambridge the Belcher family
had been accustomed to worship, we do
not know. With the Governor's family,
also, the young minister was as intimate
as with the Governor himself, and on the
14ᵗʰ of February, 1733, Mather Byles
married, no doubt with his patron's high
approval, the governor's niece, a young
widow, M.ʳˢ Anna Noyes Gale.

One of the most important gentlemen
in Boston shortly before this time, a man

who stood quite as high socially as Governor Belcher, was Doctor Oliver Noyes, son of John and Sarah Oliver Noyes, a physician practising in Boston and Medford, a graduate of Harvard of the class of 1695. Though a busy man in his profession, Doctor Noyes shared actively in all the local enterprises calculated to develop Boston, a conspicuous one of these being the building of the famous "Long Wharf." The first wife of Doctor Noyes was Ann Belcher, a younger sister of the governor, who bore her husband six children, the eldest of these being Doctor Byles's wife. Anna Noyes was born April 17, 1704, and January 31, 1722, was married to Azor Gale, Jr., of a Marblehead family, but her young husband did not live long, and as we have said, on the 14th of February, 1733, in her twenty-ninth year, she once more entered wedlock as the wife of Rev. Mather Byles. During his socially brilliant but politically turbulent eleven years' administration of the government of Massachusetts, Governor Belcher may have lived in summer in his house in Orange Street, in the south suburbs, and in winter in the Province House in town, for the marriage of his niece Anna, whose father was dead, and who was thus probably much under her uncle's care, to Mather Byles, took place in the magnificent official residence of the Massachusetts governors.[15] Weird tales, as we know, weird and impossible tales, were woven by Hawthorne about this same famous Province House, and it is pleasant in contrast to picture to ourselves the festive scene of a wedding in the official mansion. The Province House had been acquired by the Massachusetts government from the heirs of the original owner, Peter Sergeant, and when it was bought no pains had been spared to make it an elegant official residence. The house, which stood a little back from what is now Wash-

ington Street, almost opposite the Old
South Church, was of brick, three stories
high, and was approached by a stone
pavement, which led to a flight of massive
red freestone steps, and these to a door-
way, which Shurtleff in his "Topographical
and Historical Description of Boston,"
with pardonable enthusiasm declares might
have rivalled the doorways of the palaces
of Europe.   Trees of very large size, giving
abundant shade, stood in front of the house
and added much to its external attractiveness.   Inside, as a setting for the Gale-
Byles wedding, we have alluring visions
of broad staircases, carved balustrades,
escutcheon-decorated walls, more or less
valuable family portraits,[16] rich carpets,
and finely carved mahogany tables and
chairs.   Into the great state chamber,
where vice-regal levees were always held,
a wide double door gave entrance, and
there we see also among other things the
chimney piece, set round with blue-figured

PROVINCE HOUSE

Dutch porcelain tiles, which so attracted the attention of Hawthorne, who when the old Province House had come to be a humble tavern wrote the stories in which it figures, in his "Twice Told Tales." Unless the wedding in question was an entirely private ceremony, to the function would naturally have come the very flower of the Boston aristocracy of the day, for the bride and groom were both scions of families recognized as of the highest local importance, and we may be sure that Governor Belcher's "opulence" and his taste for magnificent display would have made this wedding in the gubernatorial mansion, where so many brilliant functions had already taken place, one of the finest social affairs of the year. Of the relatives of the young bride and groom, the bride's brother, Belcher Noyes was probably there, and also her sister Sarah, who had married a Pulsifer of Plymouth. The Governor's son Andrew, a graduate of Harvard of 1724,

who later married Emilia Louisa Teal of
New Jersey, daughter of his father's second
wife by her first husband, and lived in
Milton in fine style, was no doubt a guest.
The Governor's daughter Sarah, who had
been married between five and six years
before to Mr. Byfield Lyde, with her
husband was surely present, and Doctor
Byles's mother Elizabeth, then well on
towards seventy, his aunts, Maria Mather,
wife of Richard Fifield, and Sarah Mather,
wife of Rev. Nehemiah Walter of Roxbury
were probably. there; and most naturally
some of Mather Byles's cousins, the remaining children of his uncle Cotton,
notably Rev. Doctor Samuel Mather, who
a little later married a sister of Governor
Thomas Hutchinson.   Other Belchers, and
Byfields, and Lydes, and no doubt some
of the Hutchinsons probably graced the
event, and although the wedding was of
a young Congregational widow to a young
Congregational parson, the Rev. Thomas

Prince of the Old South performing the service, it is possible that the aristocratic King's Chapel congregation was almost as liberally represented as that of the Old South or the Old North.

The social history of Boston in the long Provincial period, before the Revolution came to change to a democracy the whole aristocratic structure of the popular life, has never yet with any fulness been portrayed. Important fragmentary glimpses we get of the life at various epochs, in brief descriptions of visiting Englishmen or through the diaries and letters of a few citizens, but for the most part we are left to reconstruct it in our own imaginations, as we are obliged to do that of New York or Philadelphia, or the still more intensely dramatic plantation life of the South in the same and at a later period. After the Revolution the only town on the continent where the chief features of this life were strongly perpetuated was Halifax,

Nova Scotia, where the Boston Tories all found temporary shelter and where many of them permanently remained, where through a thriving West Indian trade considerable fortunes were able to be accumulated, where the presence of the army and navy, in even greater force, indeed, than had ever been true of Boston, added the peculiar picturesqueness that has always belonged to important military and naval stations of the British Empire, and where dignified old-world class distinctions were, until beyond the period of Confederation, and to the natural dispersion of many of the older families, unchallengedly maintained.

Of Boston social life generally among the upper classes at the time of Doctor Byles's marriage, we have in our minds a pretty clear picture. Mʳ Joseph Bennett, an English traveller, in 1740 wrote an animated history of New England, with an account of his travels here, in which he describes it with a good deal of minuteness. "There are several families in Boston," he says, "that keep a coach and pair of horses; but for chaises and saddlehorses, considering the bulk of the place they outdo London. They have some nimble, lively horses for the coach, but not any of that beautiful large black breed so common in London. . . . The gentlemen ride out here as in England, some in chaises, and others on horseback, with their negroes to attend them. They travel in much the same manner on business as for pleasure, and are attended in both by their black equipages. . . . For their domestic amusements, every afternoon, after drinking tea, the gentlemen and ladies walk the Mall, and from thence adjourn to one another's houses to spend the evening, — those that are not disposed to attend the evening lecture; which they may do, if they please, six nights in seven, the year round.

E

"What they call the Mall is a walk on a fine green Common adjoining to the southwest side of the town. It is near half a mile over, with two rows of young trees planted opposite to each other, with a fine footway between, in imitation of St. James's Park; and part of the bay of the sea which encircles the town, taking its course along the north-west side of the Common, — by which it is bounded on the one side, and by the country on the other, — forms a beautiful canal, in view of the walk.

"The government being in the hands of dissenters, they don't admit of plays or music-houses. . . . But, notwithstanding plays and such like diversions do not obtain here, they don't seem to be dispirited nor moped for want of them; for both the ladies and gentlemen dress and appear as gay, in common, as courtiers in England on a coronation or birthday. And the ladies here visit, drink tea, and indulge every little piece of gentility, to the height of the mode; and neglect the affairs of their families with as good a grace as the finest ladies in London." [17]

"These people have the air of having been bred at courts," some other English visitor to Boston writes home, "where did they get it?" and a more recent writer in the "Dictionary of National Biography," sketching the life of John Singleton Copley, describes the Boston society to which Copley belonged as "composed of remarkable elements, in which learning and general culture, statesmanship, and business capacity, borrowed refinement from the presence of many women conspicuous for beauty and accomplishments." In his able "History of King's Chapel," Rev. Henry Wilder Foote suggests to us the fashion and wealth of the pre-Revolutionary congregation of that historic church. He gives us glimpses of the Royal Governors in their pew of state, hung with red cur-

tains, and raised several steps above the
floor, as it stood under the south gallery;
of the uniformed officers of the British
army and navy who for many years came
here to pray; and of the aristocratic
native-born worshippers, in brocade and
velvet, in ruffles and lace, — the Apthorps,
and Royalls, and Vassals, and Wentworths,
— who with dignified bearing and reverent
mien trod the church's aisles, and knelt
for worship in its square pews.

To the conspicuous richness of the Boston people's dress in the Provincial period
we are well introduced by Copley's portraits, as Mr. Frank W. Bayley of the
"Copley Gallery" has described them.
John Amory, senior, for example, appears
in his portrait in a gold-laced brown velvet
coat, M⁣ʳˢ Amory in rich yellow satin or
silk. M⁣ʳˢ John Apthorp is arrayed in
blue silk, edged at the neck with white
lace. She wears also a pink scarf, fastened
at the waist by a pearl pin, and has a

collar of three rows of pearls round her
neck. Mrs John Barrett has on a robe of
olive brown brocaded damask. Thomas
Aston Coffin, as a child, is dressed in a
low-necked sacque of green satin, over a
dress of white satin, richly embroidered
with lace, and has a hat with plumes.
Timothy Fitch is arrayed in a gold-laced
coat and waistcoat, and silk stockings.
Mrs Fitch is in purplish pink satin, with
blue lining. Mrs John Forbes is dressed
in yellow satin, ornamented with silver
lace, the short sleeves of her gown edged
with rich lace. She wears a large hoop,
her hair, decorated with a white bow, is
dressed over a cushion, and she has on a
necklace and earrings of pearls. Anne
Gardiner, who married Captain the Honourable Arthur Browne, wears a white
satin dress trimmed with pearls, and holds
in her left hand a pink silk mantle. Moses
Gill wears a dark blue velvet coat, lined
with white satin, and like many of Copley's

men has a powdered wig. The first Mrs Gill, a daughter, by the way, of Rev. Thomas Prince, is in dark blue velvet, with muslin undersleeves, ending in double ruffles, and she too has pearls on her neck. The second Mrs Gill, a daughter of Thomas Boylston, has on blue velvet or satin, with a red velvet band embroidered with gold around the bosom. Harrison Gray, the noted Loyalist, is painted in brown velvet, with lace at the wrists and neck, and wears a gray wig, with a queue.

That young Mather Byles's bride Anna was not the clergyman's first love we are led to believe from one of the well-known witticisms perpetrated by Byles probably soon after, or perhaps even before, he left college. Indeed it would be rather strange if she had been, for at the time of his marriage the susceptible young gentleman had reached the age of almost twenty-six. The pun we refer to was on his own and another distinguished name in Boston, and the quick retort it called forth showed that others of his contemporaries had a measure of the ready humour in which Byles excelled. It is said that one day meeting a lady to whom he had previously paid court unsuccessfully, and who was then married or about to be married to a Quincy, Byles said jocosely: "I see, Madam, that you prefer the Quincy to Byles." "Yes," the lady is reported promptly to have answered, "for if there were any ailment worse than *biles* God would have afflicted Job with it."[18] We have nowhere found it stated who the lady who was so discriminating in her choice of diseases was, but we feel very sure from our knowledge of the Quincy family and their marriages that she could have been no other than Elizabeth Wendell, who was married April 15, 1725, to Judge Edmund Quincy, and became the mother of Mrs John Hancock, the sprightly, attractive, somewhat famous lady known as

"Dorothy Q." If this was really the lady she was about three years older than Doctor Byles, and was loved by that ardent swain before he was himself eighteen.[19]

CHAPTER IV

Events in Earlier Ministry

Where Doctor Byles may have lived from the beginning of his ministry at Hollis Street Church until 1741, we do not know, but it seems quite possible that Governor Belcher may have furnished him with a house somewhere near his own. To whatever dwelling he took his bride Anna he seems also to have taken his widowed mother Elizabeth, for on the twenty-fourth of March, 1734, he records in his church register that his "aged mother" had on that day been received into communion at Hollis Street from the North Church, to which she had previously belonged.[20] A little less than three years from the beginning of his pastorate, the young minister was called to share the sorrow of his beloved patron, Governor Belcher, in the death of the latter's esteemed first wife.[21] M[rs] Belcher had apparently died at the Governor's house in Orange Street, for the *News-Letter* of October 14, 1736, intimates that her funeral procession moved for a considerable distance through the town, its statement being that along the streets through which it passed the tops of the houses and the windows were crowded with spectators. At the house, before the cortege started, the Rev. Doctor Sewall of the Old South made a prayer, and then the procession took its way through the town to the Granary Burying Ground, where the Governor in 1720 had built a tomb. The description in the *News-Letter* adds that "the coffin was covered with black velvet and richly adorned. The pall was supported by the Honourable

Dr. MATHER BYLES

From the original painting by Peter Pelham

Spencer Phipps, Esq., our Lieutenant-Governor, William Dummer, Esq., formerly Lieutenant-Governor and Commander-in-Chief of this Province, Benjamin Lynde, Esq., Thomas Hutchinson, Esq., and Adam Winthrop, Esq. His Excellency with his children and family followed the corpse, all in deep mourning; next went the several relatives according to their respective degrees, who were followed by a great many of the principal gentlewomen in town; after whom went the gentlemen of His Majesty's Council, the reverend Ministers of this and the neighbouring towns, the reverend President and fellows of Harvard College, a great number of officers both of the civil and military order, with a multitude of other gentlemen. His Excellency's coach, drawn by four horses, was covered with black cloth and adorned with escutcheons of the coats of arms both of his Excellency and of his deceased lady, and during the time of the procession the half-minute guns began, first at His Majesty's Castle William, which were followed by those on board His Majesty's ship *Squirrel*, and many other ships in the harbour, their colours being all day raised to the height, as usual on such occasions. . . . On the following Sunday his Excellency's pew and the pulpit at the South Church were put into mourning and richly adorned with escutcheons, and the Reverend Thomas Prince preached a sermon, which was printed by J. Draper, with the customary black border and death's head." [22]

In reading of this magnificent funeral display one is struck with the liberal use in it of armorial bearings, and since the governor's grandfather, Andrew Belcher of Cambridge, the first of the family in New England, was the son of a cloth-worker in London, and he the son of a weaver in Wilts, is compelled to wonder in passing where these Belcher arms were

obtained.[23] But a matter of much more
interest to our present biography is the
fact that soon after the funeral, Mather
Byles wrote an "Epistle in verse" to his
Excellency on the death of his lady, which
he piously prefaces in the following way:
"As your Excellency has long honoured
me with a particular friendship, Gratitude
demands that I attempt your Service:
and as you are now in mourning under
the Hand of God.

"In order to this, the muse has once
more resumed her Lyre, and her Aversion
to Flattery you will receive as her best
Compliment. Instead of copious Panegyric upon the Dead I have chosen rather
in solemn Language to admonish the Living; and when others perhaps would
have embraced so fair an Opportunity
for an Encomium on your Excellency, I
have only taken the Freedom of an Ex-
hortation. I know you will be pleased
to observe that while I employ the Num-

bers of the Poet, I never forget the Character of the Divine.

        "I am

    "May it please your Excellency

       "Your Excellency's

      "Affectionate Nephew and most

       " humble Servant

            "M. BYLES."

   The poem is as follows:

"Belcher, once more permit the Muse you lov'd,
By honour, and by sacred Friendship mov'd,
Wak'd by your woe, her numbers to prolong,
And pay her tribute in a Funeral song.

"From you, great Heav'n with undisputed voice
Has snatch'd the partner of your youthful joys,
Her beauties, ere slow Hectick fires consum'd,
Her eyes shone chearful, and her roses
   bloom'd:
Long lingering sickness broke the lovely form,
Shock after shock, and storm succeeding
   storm,
Till Death, relentless, seiz'd the wasting clay,
Stopt the faint voice, and catch'd the soul
   away.

"No more in Converse sprightly she appears,
With nice decorum, and obliging airs :
Ye poor, no more expecting round her stand,
Where soft compassion stretch'd her bounteous
    hand.

"Her house her happy skill no more shall boast
By all things plentiful, but nothing lost.
Cold to the tomb see the pale corpse convey'd,
Wrapt up in silence, and the dismal shade.

"Ah ! what avail the sable velvet spread,
And golden ornaments amidst the dead ?
No beam smile there, no eye can there discern
The vulgar coffin from the marble urn :
The costly honours preaching, seem to say,
'Magnificence must mingle with the clay.'

"Learn here, ye Fair, the frailty of your face,
Ravish'd by death, or nature's slow decays :
Ye Great, must so resign your transient pow'r,
Heroes of dust, and monarchs of an hour !
So must each pleasing air, each gentle fire,
And all that's soft, and all that's sweet,
    expire.

"But you, O Belcher, mourn the absent Fair,
Feel the keen pang, and drop the tender tear :

The God approves that nature do her part,
A panting bosom, and a bleeding heart:
Ye baser arts of flattery away!
The Virtuous Muse shall moralize her lay.

"To you, O Fav'rite Man, the Pow'r supream
Gives wealth and titles and extent of fame,
Joys from beneath, and blessings from above,
Thy Monarch's plaudit, and thy people's
love.

"The same high Pow'r, unbounded and alone,
Resumes his gifts, and puts your mourning on.
His Edict issues, and his Vassal *Death*,
Requires your Consort's — or Your flying
breath.

"Still be your glory at his feet to bend,
Kiss thou the Son, and own his Sovereign
hand,
For his high honours all thy pow'rs exert,
The gifts of Nature, and the charms of Art:

"So over Death the conquest shall be giv'n,
Your Name shall live on earth, your Soul in
heav'n.
Mean time my Name to *thine* ally'd shall
stand

Still our warm Friendship mutual flames ex-
    tend,
The Muse shall so survive from age to age
And Belcher's name protect his Byles's page."

In 1741 Doctor Byles bought a house of
his own and we presume immediately
moved his family into it. Within ten
years, or a little more, of her marriage,
Anna Gale had borne her second husband
six children, the eldest of these a second
Mather, the youngest but one receiving
appropriately the name of Belcher. Of
these six children, however, only three
survived their mother,[24] who herself died
April twenty-seventh, 1744. In the *News-
Letter* of May third, 1744, it was recorded:
"Last Thursday night died, and on Monday last was decently interr'd, Mrs Anna
Byles, the amiable and Vertuous Consort
of the Rev. Mr. Byles."[25] That Doctor
Byles held his first wife in proper esteem
and reverence and that he genuinely lamented her death is shown by a sermon he

F

preached soon after her funeral, in which
he extolled her virtues and commemorated
fittingly her calm and beautiful end.
"Never," he said feelingly, "did these
eyes see death vanquished in a more complete manner; nor did I ever witness to
so steady and uninterrupted a peace of
mind for so long a time together, upon a
death bed before now. The king of terrors
lay contemptible at the feet of this truly
Christian heroine. Her speeches were
wonderful and glorious. . . . She said
(the most joyful words to me that ever I
heard, before a room full of witnesses,
else I think that I should not so publicly
mention it, though she had often spoken
the same thing to me alone), 'I bless God
that I ever saw you: the doctrines of
grace, in the comforts of which I die,
have been more clearly explained and
applied to my heart under your preaching, and in your conversation, than ever
they were by any one else. And I say

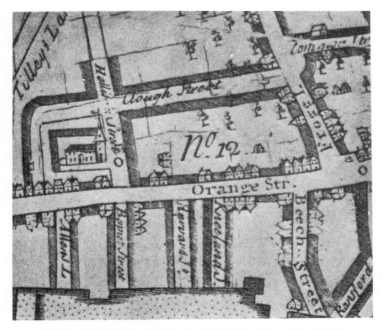

FROM BONNER'S MAP OF BOSTON, 1769, SHOWING
HOLLIS ST. CHURCH

this for your encouragement in your ministry.'"

Although the bereaved minister had young children to be cared for, and his own personal comfort to regard, he waited a little over three years before marrying again, then on the 11ᵗʰ of June, 1747, the Reverend Joseph Sewall, D.D., of the Old South officiating, he married a second wife, Rebecca Tailer, daughter of the distinguished Honourable William Tailer, deceased,[26] a lady not less highly connected than his first wife, for her father, who was a gentleman of family and fortune, had twice been lieutenant-governor of Massachusetts, and once acting governor, and had long lived in fine style in Dorchester, where he had a handsome country seat. By this marriage Doctor Byles allied himself with another considerable group of aristocratic families, for the Tailers were connected with the Brinleys, Byfields, Cradocks, Dudleys, and

Lydes, the interrelationship among which pre-Revolutionary Boston first families is such an intricate tangle that no one who had not much genealogical skill could possibly make it out. To the conspicuous names we have just given should be added also the Royalls and Boylstons, for shortly after the Tailer-Byles marriage, occurred that of Rebecca Tailer's brother, Doctor Gillam Tailer, with Elizabeth Boylston, and of her sister Abigail to Jacob Royall, Esq.

The house bought by Doctor Byles in 1741, which was destined to be his home for the rest of his own life and the home of his unmarried daughters, the Misses Mary and Catherine Byles, until their deaths, respectively in 1832 and 1837, was a plain wooden, perhaps gambrel-roofed, house which stood endwise to the street, on the site of the building known as the "Children's Mission," and its door-yard, on Tremont Street nearly opposite the entrance to Common Street. The

land on which the house stood was purchased by Peter Harratt, a bricklayer,
from Governor Belcher, in 1732, and the
house was probably erected soon after
by the buyer. Before 1741 Harratt died
and in that year his widow Catherine
sold it to Doctor Byles.[27] The house is
described in an "instructive and amusing"
game called "Cards of Boston," [28] printed
in 1831 by Miss Eliza Leslie of Philadelphia, as "a very ancient frame building
at the corner of Nassau and Tremont
streets," the outside nearly black, standing in a green inclosure, shaded with large
trees. Probably in the very year she
printed the game, Miss Leslie, a writer of
some local reputation, sister of the painter
Charles Robert Leslie, visited Boston, and
in 1842 in *Graham's Magazine* gave an
entertaining description of the house both
without and within, and of its quaint
owners, the then aged daughters of Doctor
Byles. "After passing the beautiful Com-

mon," Miss Leslie says, "my companion pointed out to me at what seemed the termination of the long vista of Tremont Street, an old black-looking frame house, which at the distance from whence I saw it seemed to block up the way by standing directly across it. It was the ancient residence of Mather Byles, and the present dwelling of his aged daughters, one of whom was in her eighty-first and the other in her seventy-ninth year. This part of Tremont Street, which is on the south-eastern declivity of a hill, carried us far from all vicinity to the aristocratic section of Boston. At length we arrived at the domain of the two antique maidens. It was surrounded by a board fence which had once been a very close one, but time and those universal depredators 'the boys' had made numerous cracks and chinks in it. The house (which stood with the gable end to the street) looked as if it had never been painted in its life. Its expos-

ure to the sun and rain, to the heats of a
hundred summers and the snows of a
hundred winters, had darkened its whole
outside nearly to the blackness of iron.
Also, it had even in its best days been
evidently one of the plainest and most
unbeautified structures in the town of
Boston, where many of the old frame
houses can boast of a redolence of quaint
ornament about the doors and windows
and porches and balconies. Still there
was something not unpleasant in its aspect,
or rather its situation. It stood at the
upper end of a green lot, whose long thick
grass was enamelled with field flowers.
It was shaded with noble horse-chestnut
trees relieved against the clear blue sky,
and whose close and graceful clusters of
long jagged leaves, fanned by the light
summer breeze, threw their chequered and
quivering shadows on the grass beneath
and on the mossy roof of the venerable
mansion." The house, Miss Leslie further

minutely tells her readers, was a gambrel-
roofed house, which when Tremont Street
was extended beyond its original terminus
had had a piece taken off its southeastern
end or "side."

After Doctor Byles's second marriage
there soon appeared in succession in the
Tremont Street house, three more children,
whom their parents named respectively,
Joseph, Mary, and Catherine,[29] the first
of these like several of his little half
brothers dying young, the second and
third, however, the Misses Mary and
Catherine Byles, living far beyond the
Revolution, until they had become very
old. The second wife of Doctor Byles,
of whom we have very little knowledge,
lived until July twenty-third, 1779, when
she too, as we learn from her daughters'
wills, was buried in tomb No. 2 in the
Granary Burying Ground. That both
Doctor Byles's marriages were as happy
as marriages commonly are we have no

reason not to suppose. At the time of the Revolution, when the Doctor was in sore disgrace politically in the town, a young minister, John Eliot, with youthful censoriousness, and with evident familiarity with the town's gossip, is reported to have said that "the women all proclaimed " [30] that the misfortunes that had come upon Doctor Byles were a judgment on him from Heaven for his bad treatment of his wives, but this gratuitous fling is the sole reflection of the kind we have ever seen made on Mather Byles.

CHAPTER V

ON the long active ministry of Mather
Byles at Hollis Street, which terminated
really though not formally when the occu-
pation of Boston by the British in the
Revolution sent the greater part of his
parishioners out of the town, we have
considerable light. The facts we have,
however, are chiefly of the ordinary details
of parochial administration and of sermons
preached year after year, many of which,
soon after preaching, Doctor Byles put
into print. The Hollis Street congregation was never an influential congregation
like the congregations of the First Church
or the Old South, though from the start
it had on its communion roll many respectable names,[31] but we have every reason to

74

Thomas Hollis late of London Merch.ᵗ a most generous Benefactor to Harvard College, in N.E. having founded two Professorships and ten Scholarships in the said College, given a fine Apparatus for Experimental Philosophy & increased the Library with a large Number of valuable Books &.

believe that Doctor Byles's ministry to his parishioners was earnest, faithful, sympathetic, and kind.

In spite of his intellectual activity and general learning, Mather Byles made no original contribution to New England theology. The period his ministry covered, indeed, was one not of entire theological inactivity but certainly of marked lack of constructive energy in theological and theologico-political things. The work of shaping Congregationalism, in which those stern theocrats, his great-grandfathers John Cotton and Richard Mather had borne chief parts, had long been accomplished, the dispute over the half-way covenant had lost much of its original fervour, the political and religious indignation which had been visited on Increase Mather on his return from England because of the defects of the Charter of 1691 had subsided like other similar indignations, and the only remarkable stir-

ring of the Boston churches until the
Revolution was the Great Awakening under
Whitefield in 1740–'42. The period of
Doctor Byles's ministry is described by
New England church historians as on the
whole one of comparative formalism and
general lack of spiritual enthusiasm. During the time, however, religious thought
was not inactive, religious thought never
stands entirely still, under the leadership
of a series of strenuous thinkers it was
moving quietly in two opposite ways. Of
these two movements the most striking
was what is known as Hopkinsianism,
which affirmed as Calvinistic logic had
never done before the absolute sover-
eignty of God, and the necessity for un-
conditional submission, even to the point
of willingness to be damned for his glory,
of the human soul to Him. At the opposite
pole from this tremendous irrationalism
was the moderate assertion of the validity
of human reason, of Chauncy, Mayhew,

Briant, and others, of eastern Massachusetts, an assertion which was to strengthen
and grow until the beginning of the nineteenth century, when Unitarianism, fully
developed, should come into existence
through those able rational leaders Chan-
ning and Ware. But the thought of by
far the larger number in the period
of Byles's life ran on what is properly
called "Old Calvinist" lines. The familiar doctrines of man's depravity, inherited
from fallen Adam, redemption through
the sacrificial death of Christ, and the
arbitrary bestowal by God of divine grace
to bring about repentance in the elect, —
these conventional tenets of Calvinism
were tenaciously but conservatively held.[32]
But the further belief was held by the
Old Calvinists that however fixed by eternal decrees the fate of men might be, the
common means of grace, prayer, reading
of Scripture, and attendance on preaching,
honestly used "put men in a favourable

way for obtaining the more special and
effectual bestowments of divine help es-
sential to salvation," [33] and to this Old
Calvinist party Doctor Byles emphatically
belonged.   Reading his sermons one finds
in him absolutely no traces of a disposition
towards the extreme views of Hopkins,
nor does the least tendency appear towards
Unitarian thought, but he everywhere affirms the main positions of Calvinism,
and with apparently entirely unquestion-
ing faith.   In the common view of his
day that from beginning to end the Scriptures were the inerrant message of God he
profoundly shared, but as in politics so
in religion his attitude was essentially non-
controversial, and his chief aim in preaching was to bring what he conceived to be
the teaching of the Scriptures with con-
vincing power to the practical life of men.
With a narrower range of intellectual interests than his uncle Cotton Mather, he
yet shared unmistakably in the peculiar

mental temperament of his uncle, but although he had as unwavering confidence in the value of saintly death-bed experiences and with as fervid imagination revelled in the unspeakable glories of the unseen Heaven where after death the chosen saints were to go, he yet escaped the amazing credulity of Cotton Mather and showed little of the superstition that characterized that extraordinary man. For the most part the style of his sermons is simple and direct. Occasionally, overpowered by his subject he indulges in the strained elegance of fine writing, but generally his writing, while not at all lacking in smoothness, is remarkably forceful and clear. To these merits of expression he often adds the power of a rich and vivid imagination, and we can well understand how with a magnetic presence in the pulpit and a musical voice he quickly earned for himself the reputation of a brilliant preacher.

As we review, even hastily, the sermons
and essays of Doctor Byles, written during
his pastorate, that have been printed,
as indeed his poetry throughout his life,
we cannot help regretting that after his
death some kind friend had not cared
enough for him to collect his writings
into two or three volumes, for some of
his productions, both in prose and poetry,
are of lasting interest.   In the next chapter
we shall speak of the fine imagination displayed in his noble sermon on "The Flourish of the Annual Spring," we cannot
refrain from giving here an extract printed
by Duyckinck, in his "Cyclopædia of
American Literature," from his essay,
"The Meditation of Cassim, the Son of
Ahmed," first printed in the *New England
Weekly Journal* some time in 1727, and
afterward reprinted in 1771 with the second
edition of his sermon on "The Present
Vileness of the Body and Its Future
Glorious Change by Christ," from Acts

17 : 18. Speaking of the worm changing into a butterfly Byles says: "You have beheld the dead Silk-worm revive a Butterfly, the most beautiful and curious of all the splendid Race of Insects. What more entertaining Specimen of the Resurrection is there, in the whole Circumference of Nature? Here are all the wonders of the Day in Miniature. It was once a despicable Worm, it is raised a kind of painted little Bird. Formerly it crawled along with a slow and leisurely Motion: now it flutters aloft upon its guilded Wings. How much improved is its speckled Covering, when all the Gaudiness of Colour is scattered about its Plumage. It is spangled with Gold and Silver, and has every Gem of the *Orient* sparkling among its Feathers. Here a brilliant spot, like a clear Diamond, twinkles with an unsullied Flame, and trembles with num'rous Lights, that glitter in a gay Confusion. There a Saphire casts a milder Gleam, and shows like the

G

blue Expanse of Heaven in a fair Winter
Evening. In this Place an Emerald, like
the calm Ocean, displays its cheerful and
vivid Green. And close by a Ruby —
flames with the ripened Blush of the
Morning. The Breast and Legs, like
Ebony, shine with a glorious Darkness;
while its expanded Wings are edged with
the golden Magnificence of the Topaz.
Thus the illustrious little creature is furnished with the divinest Art, and looks
like an animated Composition of Jewels,
that blend their promiscuous Beams about
him. Thus O *Cassim*, shall the Bodies of
Good Men be raised; thus shall they
shine, and thus fly away."

That the "Great Awakening" of 1740–
'42 influenced very deeply the Hollis Street
Church or its pastor we have no reason to
think, for the records of the Church during
that time do not show any very remarkable
increase in the number of admissions to
communion.[34] When Whitefield first ap-

peared in Boston in the middle of September, 1740, he was received generally
among Congregationalists, and no doubt
by Doctor Byles as by other ministers,
with great warmth and was heartily welcomed to the churches. On the 26th of
the month he preached from a scaffold
erected outside the Hollis Street meeting-
house, no doubt to accommodate a larger
audience than could find room within the
building. From a discussion in 1743 of
the effects of the revival in which several
ministers took an earnest part, some ap-
proving, others deprecating, Doctor Byles
and his cousin Samuel Mather, with two
other ministers, Mr Welsteed and Mr
Gray, stood entirely aloof. In the councils
of the denomination to which he belonged,
called for the installation or dismissal of
ministers or for other reasons, the Hollis
Street Church and its pastor are frequently
mentioned, as on the 18th of May, 1768,
when the Rev. John Lathrop was ordained

pastor of the Second Church. On that occasion the young pastor himself preached the ordination sermon, Doctor Joseph Sewall offered prayer, Rev. Ebenezer Pemberton gave the charge, and Doctor Byles gave the right hand of fellowship. In March, 1740, Doctor Byles offered the prayer at a Town Meeting, in the same year he delivered the sermon before the Artillery Company, and probably many times he preached the "Thursday Lecture" in the First Church, which had been established by his great-grandfather John Cotton, and which has continued to be preached almost continuously to the present time.[35]   That like his son Mather Byles, Jr., and his daughters, in spite of his strong Toryism, Doctor Byles had, even after the Revolution, any desire to become an Anglican we have seen no evidence.   He was too near the old New England Puritan theocracy, and the influence of the Mather dynasty was probably too strong upon his mind to admit of his having much sympathy with Anglican ecclesiasticism, however much he may have sympathized with Anglicans socially, in Old England or New.

In 1765, Doctor Byles received the degree of Doctor of Divinity from the University of Aberdeen, another Boston minister, the Rev. Jonathan Mayhew of the West Church, also having received a similar honour from this university fifteen years before.[36] Shortly after the news of the conferring of his degree reached him, he wrote the Rev. Doctor John Chalmers, "Principal of King's College and University," in which he acknowledges the honour that had been done him, and says that he had been trying to collect his published writings to send to the university library. This letter, which we have permission to print, is found in an old letter-book of Doctor Byles's, owned by the New England Historic Genealogical Society. It reads as follows:

"To the Revd Doctor John Chalmers Principal of the King's College and University at
Aberdeen.

"REV'D SIR,

"The honour which the University of Aberdeen has done me, and your good offices in
particular, call for my Respectful Acknowledgements. I have endeavour'd to collect the
Publications I have made, to send as a small
Tribute to the Publick Library : but I have
been able to procure but few, the rest, though
some of them have past several Editions, being
wholly out of Print. I hope they will have a
little more to recommend them, than as Trifling
curiosities from a Far Country. Wishing you,
and the Illustrious University, every Favour of
Heaven, and asking your Prayers and Blessings,
                    "I am
              "your dutiful Son,
                "and most obliged
                  "humble Servant."

Doctor Byles's aristocratic tendencies,
and the important social position he himself held in Boston, as we have previously
said, were of themselves calculated to

arouse antagonism against him in the minds of his more democratic brother ministers of Massachusetts, and in the feeling of many of the faithful laity as well. In the autumn of 1741, Rev. Eleazer Wheelock, one of the founders of Dartmouth College, visited Boston, and under date of October 9th., evidently with enormous self-satisfaction, writes in his diary: "Preached [in the Old South Church] to a very thronged assembly, many more than could get into the house, with very great freedom and enlargement. I believe the children of God were very much refreshed. They told me afterwards they believed that Mather Byles was never so lashed in his life." Precisely why the "children of God" of the Old South Church should have been so delighted to see Byles "lashed," or Doctor Eleazer Wheelock to have "lashed" him, particularly at this early period of Byles's ministry, so long before his political opinions had become offensive, it is not easy now to tell, but that censorious younger ministers like John Eliot and Jeremy Belknap should habitually have sneered at and ridiculed him, as they did, argues chiefly the strength of his personality, the variety of his gifts, and the superior position in the community he held. That he was unpopular among certain classes of laymen in Boston may be due largely to the fact that he did not strictly bind his conduct by all the conventions that had been established for men of his profession, and that he never hesitated to give voice to his opinions, whether they agreed with those of the majority or not.

After the dissolution of his pastorate of the Hollis Street Church Doctor Byles probably saw very little of his former Congregational friends of the clergy or the laity. Many of his most intimate associates had been among the Royalists, and these had all been compelled to leave

the town. The worthy people who now
filled public positions and constituted the
town's society for the most part despised
and shunned him, and he in return came
near to despising them, and he almost
certainly kept pretty closely to the society
of his daughters and a very few other
persons who, whether sharing his political
sympathies or not, still remained loyally
his friends. Had he been a younger man
he would without doubt have been driven
into exile with his son and the rest of
the Tories, but he was too old voluntarily
to remove from Boston, and the house
in Tremont Street where he lived, with
its contents, was almost all he owned
in the world. If he now regularly attended any religious service it was probably the service of the Anglican Trinity
Church, into full communion with which
his daughters either before or shortly
after the Revolution entered. One intimate friend, however, in these years he

had among the younger Congregational
ministers of Massachusetts, the Rev. Nathaniel Emmons of Wrentham, whom Doctor Leonard Woods credited with having
"one of the grandest understandings ever
created." Doctor Emmons was thirty-
eight years younger than Doctor Byles,
but from about 1770 to the death of the
latter in 1788 the two were deeply at-
tached friends. "The parson was one of
my best friends," Doctor Emmons is
quoted as saying on one occasion, "and I
don't know but I owe more to him than
to any other man I ever knew; for it was
he who taught me never to preach what
I did not fully believe, and that it is no
certain mark of godliness to wear a sad
countenance. In fact he once told me
that the genuine Christian denied his
profession if he was not continually jolly,
for his 'calling and èlection' being sure
he had no occasion to feel any anxiety
on any subject whatever." "Doctor

Byles was one of the best and purest men that ever lived." [37]

That Doctor Byles was especially interested in natural science, and antiquarian research, and gave a good deal of attention to these studies, notices of his collection of curiosities, and incidental references in his sermons, and articles enumerated in the inventory of his effects made after his death, sufficiently˜ show. Among these effects were geographical maps, many perspective glasses, microscopes, mathematical instruments, globes, a microscope pyramid, solar pyramid, universal pyramid, an opaque pyramid, a magic lanthorn and apparatus, a prism, camera obscura, pyramidical camera, "turcle" shell burning glass, thermometers and a barometer, half-hour glasses, reflecting telescopes, silver coins, and valuable prints. According to the inventory, his library numbered in all 2,806 books, valued at a hundred and forty-two pounds, twelve shillings, and tenpence.

CHAPTER VI

Doctor Byles as a Poet

Doctor Byles's prose writing, as we have said, is almost without exception of a high order, and it would be interesting, if we could, to give wider extracts from it here than our space will allow. His poetry varies much in excellence, but a few of his poems have an exaltation of spirit and a beauty of form that make them well worthy to be remembered. In 1736, Byles published a small 18$^{mo.}$ volume of verse, of a hundred and eighteen pages, which bore the modest title, "Poems on Several Occasions, by Mr Byles." In the preface to this volume the author explains to us that the poems "had for the most part been written as the amusements of looser hours, while the author belonged

to the college and was unbending his mind
from severer studies in the entertainment
of the classics." Most of them, it con-
tinues, had been several times printed in
Boston, in London, and elsewhere, either
separately or in miscellanies, and were
now drawn together in print for the first
time. In printing them, the author says,
"he gives up at once these lighter productions and bids adieu to the airy Muse."
The volume presents us with a considerable
variety of verse, a number of hymns,
verses written in a copy of Milton's
"Paradise Lost," a poem to the memory
of a young commander slain in battle
with the Indians in 1724, a poem to an
ingenious young gentleman on his dedicat-
ing a poem to the author, a poem to
Pictorio on the sight of his pictures, and
verses addressed to Doctor Isaac Watts
and others.

Two years after Byles left college, in
August, 1727, news reached Boston that

King George the First had died in June
at Osnaburg, in Westphalia, and that
George the Second had ascended the
throne, and Byles wrote a poem on the
double event surcharged with panegyric.
Of the dead king he writes:

"He dies! let nature own the direful blow,
  Sigh all ye winds, with tears ye rivers flow,
  Let the wide ocean loud in anguish roar,
  And tides of grief pour plenteous on the shore;
  No more the spring shall bloom, or morning
      rise,
  But night eternal wrap the sable skies."

But, the king is dead, long live the king!
and the laureate proceeds:

"Enough, my muse, give all thy tears away,
  Break ye dull shades, and rise the rosey day,
  Quicken, O Sun, thy Chariot dazzling-bright,
  And o'er thy flaming empire pour the light,
  O Spring, along thy laughing lawns be seen
  Fields alway fresh, and groves forever green,
  Let Britain's sorrows cease, her joys inlarge,
  The first revives within the second George."

On the 13ᵗʰ of July, 1728, Governor William Burnet arrived at Boston, in great state, from New York, to assume the government of Massachusetts. "He was welcomed with more of pomp and parade," says Doctor George Ellis, "than had ever been observed in Boston on any previous occasion, and at an expense to the treasury of eleven hundred pounds. There was a cavalcade, lavish festivity, and a poetical rhapsody anticipating the 'soaring eagle' style, by the famous Mather Byles." This poem was published in the *New England Weekly Journal*, but later Byles must have written another, for we have one not published in this newspaper which begins as follows :

"Welcome great man to our desiring eyes ;
Thou earth proclaim it and resound ye skies !
Voice answering Voice, in joyful Concert meet,
The Hills all echo, and the Rocks repeat ;
And Thou, O Boston, Mistress of the Towns,
Whom the pleased Bay with am'rous Arms surrounds,

"Let thy warm Transports blaze in num'rous
    Fires,
  And beaming Glories glitter on thy Spires;
  Let Rockets, streaming, up the Ether glare,
  And flaming Serpents hiss along the Air.
  While rising shouts a gen'ral Joy proclaim,
  And ev'ry tongue, O Burnet, lisps thy Name."

In 1729 (May 19), Byles first published,
in the *New England Weekly Journal*, a
noted poem of his that eventually bore
the elaborate title, "The Conflagration,
applied to that Grand Period or Catastrophe of our World, when the face of
Nature is to be changed by a Deluge of
Fire as formerly it was by that of Water.
The God of Tempest and Earthquake."
In a note introducing it in the *Journal*,
it is said that the author wrote the poem
when he was only in his fifteenth year.
If this is true, Byles's poetical genius indeed flowered early, for the poem is a
strong one, showing traces of the influence
of Milton perhaps, but indicating a native

power of imagination and sense of discrimination in the use of words that would stamp any youth as giving great promise in the field of poetical composition. Some of the lines are as follows:

"But O! what sounds are able to convey
The wild confusions of the dreadful day!
Eternal mountains totter on their base,
And strong convulsions work the valley's
    face;
Fierce hurricanes on sounding pinions soar,
Rush o'er the land, on the toss'd billows roar,
And dreadful in resistless eddies driven,
Shake all the crystal battlements of heaven.
See the wild winds, big blustering in the air,
Drive through the forests, down the mountains
    tear,
Sweep o'er the valleys in their rapid course,
And nature bends beneath the impetuous force.
Storms rush at storms, at tempests tempests
    roar,
Dash waves on waves, and thunder to the
    shore.
Columns of smoke on heavy wings ascend,
And dancing sparkles fly before the wind.

H

Devouring flames, wide-waving, roar aloud,
And melted mountains flow a fiery flood :
Then, all at once, immense the fires arise,
A bright destruction wraps the crackling skies ;
While all the elements to melt conspire,
And the world blazes in the final fire."

In 1732 Governor Belcher's brother-in-law, Hon. Daniel Oliver, died, and Doctor Byles addressed to His Excellency an elegiac poem on the melancholy event. On the 6th of October, 1736, as we have already shown, he indited a laudatory epistle in verse to the governor on the death of Mrs. Belcher, and in 1737, when Queen Caroline departed this life, he again addressed his patron in a poem.

In 1744 appeared a "Collection of Poems by Several Hands," which was evidently, as Moses Coit Tyler says, the offspring of an amiable conspiracy on the part of a group of literary friends of Doctor Byles, among them Rev. John Adams, to accomplish, and with Byles's own entire approbation, the apotheosis of the Hollis Street parson, and to induce the public to believe that one of Boston's most gifted preachers was likewise a great poet. One of these adulatory poems addresses Byles in the following style :

"Hail charming poet, whose distinguished lays
    Excite our wonder and surmount our praise,
Whom all the muses with fresh ardour fire,
And Aganippe's chrystal streams inspire."

Another describes Byles as "Harvard's honour and New England's hope," declares that he

"Bids fair to rise and sing and rival Pope,"

and informs the world that

"Could Janus live again, he'd wish to die,
    If in oblivion Byles would let him ly."

Still another sings :

"Long has New England groan'd beneath the
    Load
Of too too just Reproaches from Abroad,

Unlearn'd in Arts, and barren in their Skill
How to employ the tender Muses Quill:
At length our Byles aloft transfers his name,
And binds it on the radient wings of fame;
All we could wish the Youth he now appears,
A finish'd Poet in his blooming years.
With anxious care we see the Stripling climb
Those Heights we deem'd for mortals too
    sublime,
And dread a dang'rous Fall . . .
Yet fondly gaze, till he, above our fears
Has lost th' attracting world and shines
    among the stars."

Whatever admirer wrote this last poem
printed it first anonymously in the *New
England Weekly Journal* of August 5, 1728.

In this collection of slightly twenty
poems, which for the most part are "little
more than weak reverberations of Pope,"
several are by Doctor Byles himself. One
of these is "The Comet," a poem having
little except smoothness to recommend it,
and another a long poem with even less
merit, describing a Harvard Commence-

67261

ment. In this description, as usual in
Pope's measure, the writer shows us the
Boston folk crowding down to the Charles
River ferry, the procession forming in the
Yard, the dignified president, the senate,
the black-coated undergraduates, and the
public, all in line, the exercises within the
chapel, and then as the crowning event of
the day, the grand Commencement Dinner.

When Doctor Byles graduated from college, Alexander Pope was in the full flush
of his fame on this side of the Atlantic,
having here, as is well known, many of
his most ardent devotees. On the 7th of
October, 1727, Byles ventured to address
the great man, and his letter, the original
draft of which he preserved, shows the
supreme reverence in which he held him
and his art. "Sir," he writes, "you are
doubtless wondering at the novelty of an
epistle from the remote shores where this
dates its origin; as well as from so obscure
a hand as that which subscribes it. But

what corner of the earth so secret as not
to have heard the name of Mr. Pope?
or who so retired as not to be acquainted
with his admirable compositions, or so
stupid as not to be ravished with them. . . .
How often have I been .soothed and
charmed with the ever blooming landscape
of your *Windsor Forest!* And how does
my very Soul melt away at the soft complaints of the languishing *Eloisa!* How
frequently has the *Rape of the Lock* com-
manded the various passions of my mind,
provoked laughter, breathed a tranquillity,
or inspired a transport! And how have
I been raised and borne away by the
resistless fire of the *Iliad*, as it glows in
your immortal translation." At the close,
he begs to be permitted to conclude his
letter by "asking the favour of a few lines
from the land which has blessed the world
with such divine productions." "If you
thus honour me," he writes, "assure yourself the joys you will produce in me will

ALEXANDER POPE

From an engraving by Houbraken

be inferior to none but that Poetick Rapture of your own Breast. Perhaps you will be disposed to smile when I confess that I have a more superstitious ardour to see a word written by your Pen than ever *Tom Folio* in the Tatler to see a simile of Virgil." "Sir," he subscribes his epistle, "Your great Admirer and most obedient Humble Servant, Mather Byles."

On the 3ᵈ of May, 1728, he indites a letter to the great hymn writer, Doctor Isaac Watts, which is only a little less adoring than his letter to Pope. "Reverend and most admired Sir," he begins, "almost ever since I was first charmed well with your *Lyrick* poems I have had no little ambition to be known to you. I have often wished to do myself the honour of addressing you with a letter. But the fear which naturally seizes us when we approach great men has often prevented me." "New England," he later modestly says, "has had no great reputation of producing many fine poets, nor have we been very famous for our skill in the arts of the muses. However, so it happens that we love to be dabbling in the streams of Parnassus, though the product is nothing but muddy water."

In incidental notices of Doctor Byles in Boston print a good deal has been made of Byles's correspondence with these two noted English poets, and with a third English writer who more or less successfully cultivated the muses, George Granville or Grenville, Lord Lansdowne, who lived between 1667 and 1735.[38] With Pope, Byles's correspondence was extremely formal and rare, the little man of Twickenham, although he sent Byles (without any word whatever) a handsomely bound copy of his Odyssey when it appeared, apparently never warming very much to his transatlantic admirer.[39] With Doctor Watts, an Independent minister and a Calvinist, Byles had the bond of theological

D<small>R</small>. I<small>SAAC</small> WATTS

From an engraving by Trotter

and ecclesiastical as well as poetical sympathy, and naturally his correspondence with the noted nonconformist divine was of a much more familiar and friendly sort. Of the extent of this correspondence we are not sure, but we know that Doctor Watts sent Byles copies of some of his hymns when they appeared, and that Byles in return sent some of his poems to the English divine.   Byles's correspondence with Lansdowne probably extended only to one letter from the New England poet to the noble lord.

It is doubtful if any honour Byles ever received in his lifetime gratified him so much as the reception of Pope's Odyssey. In lending it once to a lady he accompanied it with these gallant lines of his own :

"Go, my dear Pope, transport the attentive
    fair,
And soothe with winning harmony her ear,
'Twill add new graces to thy heav'nly song
To be repeated by her gentle tongue.

Old Homer's shade shall smile if she com-
mend,
And Pope be proud to write as Byles to lend."

That Doctor Byles had given considerable attention to the *art* of poetry we have
strong testimony in a sermon he preached
at the Thursday Lecture, May third, 1739,
on "The Flourish of the Annual Spring."
This sermon, which shows probably a
finer imagination than any other he printed,
is from Canticles 2 : 10–13, "Rise up and
come away, lo the winter is past, the rain
is over and gone; the flowers appear on
the earth, the time of the singing of birds
is come. . . . Arise . . . and come away."
"Of all mere men who have lived since the
fall of Adam," the sermon begins, "the
author of this beautiful passage is pronounced the wisest by the God of Heaven.
And of all the books he wrote this is the
most elegant, sublime, and devout. The
title of the book is the Song of Songs and
it well deserves the name, for it is the

finest poetical composure now extant in the world. It is not everywhere over nice and exact in its metaphors and allusions, but they are bold and grand, elevated and lofty, all fire, all consecrated rapture and inspiration! The criticks of the Art of Poetry will presently see that it is a dramatic composition of that kind to which the moderns would give the name of a Pastoral Opera. That it is a dramatic performance is easily discovered, inasmuch as it consists wholly of action, dialogue, and character. It is a personal representation of passion and action, dialogue and history, all of which are the exact description of the drama. It is an opera, it seems to consist of three acts. The numbers are of the lyrick kind, and it has in it the evident intimations of musick and a chorus. And it is a pastoral, as the scenes are mostly laid in the country, and the characters and images are principally rural. But more than this, 'tis a

Divine Poem.   It contains a fine picture of the loves of Christ and his Church."   Soon the writer lets his fancy loose among the lovely sights and sounds and odors of the spring: "The time of the singing of birds is come, and our ears are regaled by all the harmony of the groves and forests.   The idle musicians of the spring fill the fields and the skies with their artless melody.   A thousand odours are thrown from every bough, and scatter thro' the air to gratify our smell.   The flowers appear on the earth, and the spring buds and rising grass dress the rich landscape and paint the scene to delight and charm our eyes.   These are the pleasures of an earthly spring."   Bound up with this sermon we find a musical "Hymn for the Spring," of fourteen stanzas, five of which are as follows:

"By tuneful birds of every plume
    Melodious strains are play'd,
From tree to tree their accents roam,
    Soft-warbling thro' the shade.

"The painted Meads and fragrant Fields
A sudden smile bestow,
A golden Gleam each Valley yields,
Where numerous Beauties blow.

"A Thousand gaudy Colours flush
Each od'rous Mountain's Side :
Lillies rise fair, and Roses blush
And Tulips spread their Pride.

"Thus flourishes the wanton Year,
In rich Profusion gay,
Till Autumn bids the bloom retire,
The Verdure fade away.

"Succeeding Cold withers the Woods,
While heavy Winter reigns,
In Fetters binds the frozen Floods,
And shivers o'er the Plains."

In a curious little book of sacred music,
called the "New England Psalm-Singer
or American Chorister," published by Edes
and Gill, probably in 1770, containing
"a number of psalm-tunes, anthems, and
canons, in four and five parts," composed

by William Billings of Boston, the book
including a frontispiece engraving by Paul
Revere, is a hymn by Doctor Byles, entitled "New-England Hymn [Adapted to
America Tune]."   This hymn is as follows:

"To Thee the tuneful Anthem soars,
     To Thee, our Father's God, and ours;
  This Wilderness we chose our Seat:
  To Rights secur'd by Equal Laws
  From Persecution's Iron Claws,
     We here have sought our calm Retreat.

"See! how the Flocks of Jesus rise!
  See! how the Face of Paradise
     Blooms thro' the Thickets of the Wild!
  Here Liberty erects her Throne;
  Here Plenty pours her Treasures down!
     Peace smiles, as Heav'nly Cherub mild.

"Lord, guard thy Favours; Lord, extend
  Where farther Western Suns descend;
     Nor Southern Seas the Blessings bound;
  'Till Freedom lift her chearful Head,
  'Till pure Religion onward spread,
     And beaming, wrap the Globe around."

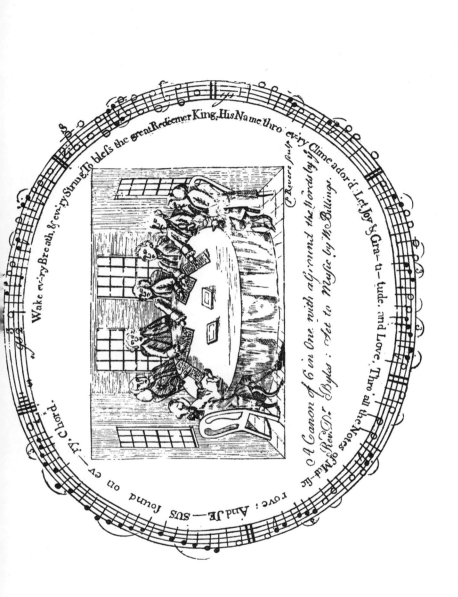

That Doctor Byles had much interest in music is shown not only by the hymn given above but by the following lines descriptive of fugue music, which appear on the tenth page of the " Psalm Singer," and are there said to be "from a miscellany of the Rev. Dr Byles " :

"Down steers the *Bass* with grave majestic Air,
And up the *Treble* mounts with shrill Career;
With softer Sounds, in mild Melodious Maze,
Warbling between, the *Tenor* gently Plays :
But if th' aspiring *Altus* join its Force,
See! like the Lark, it Wings its tow'ring
    Course;
Thro' Harmony's sublimest Sphere it flies,
And to Angelic Accents seems to rise;
From the bold Height it hails the echoing *Bass*,
Which swells to meet, and mix in close embrace.
Tho' diff'rent Systems all the Parts divide,
With Music's Chords the distant Notes are
    ty'd;
And Sympathetick Strains enchanting winde
Their restless Race, till all the Parts are join'd :
Then rolls the Rapture thro' the air around
In the full Magic Melody of Sound."

Byles's verses to Doctor Isaac Watts, in "Poems on Several Occasions," are as follows:

"To the Reverend Doctor Watts, on his Divine
    Poems.

"Say, smiling Muse, what heav'nly Strain
    Forbids the Waves to roar;
 Comes gently gliding o'er the Main,
    And charms our list'ning Shore!

"What Angel strikes the tremb'ling Strings;
    And whence the golden Sound!
 Or is it Watts — or Gabriel sings
    From yon celestial Ground?

"'Tis Thou, Seraphick Watts, thy Lyre
    Plays soft along the Floods;
 Thy Notes, the ans'ring Hills inspire,
    And bend the waving Woods.

"The Meads, with dying Musick fill'd,
    Their smiling Honours show,
 While, whisp'ring o'er each fragrant Field,
    The tuneful Breezes blow.

"The Rapture sounds in ev'ry Trace,
    Ev'n the rough Rocks regale,

Fresh flow'ry Joys flame o'er the Face
   Of ev'ry laughing Vale.

"And Thou, my Soul, the Transport own,
   Fir'd with immortal Heat;
While dancing Pulses driving on,
   About thy Body beat.

"Long as the Sun shall rear his Head,
   And chase the flying Glooms,
As blushing from his nuptial Bed
   The gallant Bridegroom comes:

"Long as the dusky Ev'ning flies
   And sheds a doubtful Light,
While sudden rush along the Skies
   The sable Shades of Night:

"O Watts, thy sacred Lays so long
   Shall ev'ry Bosom fire;
And ev'ry Muse, and ev'ry Tongue
   To speak thy Praise conspire.

"When thy fair Soul shall on the Wings
   Of shouting Seraphs rise,
And with superior Sweetness sings
   Amid thy native Skies;

I

"Still shall thy lofty Numbers flow,
  Melodious and divine;
And Choirs above, and Saints below,
  A deathless Chorus! join.

"To our far Shores the Sound shall roll
  (So *Philomela* sung),
And East to West, and Pole to Pole
  Th' eternal Tune prolong."

In the next chapter we shall speak in some detail of a passage-at-arms in wit that once took place between Byles and a rival humourist in Boston, a well-known man named Joseph Green. Doctor Byles had a favourite cat which he sometimes jocularly called his muse, and in the course of events the cat died. On its death Green, who whether chiefly from ill-will or solely from a love of practical joking seems to have lost no opportunity of ridiculing Byles, wrote and published an elegy on the cat. The absurd poem is as follows:

"Oppress'd with grief in heavy strains I mourn
The partner of my studies from me torn.

How shall I sing? what numbers shall I chuse?
For in my fav'rite cat I've lost my muse.
No more I feel my mind with raptures fir'd,
I want those airs that Puss so oft inspir'd;
No crowding thoughts my ready fancy fill,
Nor words run fluent from my easy quill;
Yet shall my verse deplore her cruel fate,
And celebrate the virtues of my cat.

"In acts obscene she never took delight;
No caterwauls disturb'd our sleep by night;
Chaste as a virgin, free from every stain,
And neighb'ring cats mew'd for her love in
vain.

"She never thirsted for the chickens' blood;
Her teeth she used only to chew her food;
Harmless as satires which her master writes,
A foe to scratching, and unused to bites,
She in the study was my constant mate;
There we together many evenings sat.
Whene'er I felt my tow'ring fancy fail,
I stroked her head, her ears, her back, and tail;
And as I stroked improv'd my dying song
From the sweet notes of her melodious tongue:
Her purrs and mews so evenly kept time,
She purr'd in metre, and she mew'd in rhyme.

But when my dulness has too stubborn prov'd,
Nor could by Puss's music be remov'd,
Oft to the well-known volumes have I gone,
And stole a line from Pope or Addison.

"Ofttimes when lost amidst poetic heat,
  She leaping on my knee has took her seat;
  There saw the throes that rock'd my lab'ring
      brain,
  And lick'd and claw'd me to myself again.

"Then, friends, indulge my grief and let me
      mourn,
  My cat is gone, ah! never to return.
  Now in my study, all the tedious night,
  Alone I sit, and unassisted write;
  Look often round (O greatest cause of pain),
  And view the num'rous labours of my brain;
  Those quires of words array'd in pompous
      rhyme,
  Which braved the jaws of all-devouring time,
  Now undefended and unwatch'd by cats
  Are doom'd a victim to the teeth of rats."

CHAPTER VII

Doctor Byles's Humour

Two ministers who filled a marked and honourable place in eighteenth century Boston, says a writer in the "Memorial History," [40] were Thomas Prince of the Old South Church, and Mather Byles of the Hollis Street Church. "Thomas Prince shares with Cotton Mather the reputation of being the most learned man in New England in the eighteenth century. He far surpassed all the Mathers in the method, accuracy, and usefulness of his writings. Mather Byles was too wayward and eccentric a genius to make a very permanent impression, though he had remarkable literary gifts, and a fancy which in his earlier years knew no bounds. He early obtained eminence in the pulpit,

and in spite of his literary interests and the
sharpness of his tongue, he maintained
cordial relations with his church until
the Revolution separated them, Doctor
Byles taking the losing side. The tradi-
tions of his overflowing wit are now the
most vivid part of his reputation, and
doubtless do less than justice to his piety,
ability, and learning." With such an estimate of Doctor Byles we partly but not
wholly agree. That his intellectual gifts
can properly be called wayward and eccentric we do not believe, but it is per-
fectly true that this brilliant descendant
of Increase Mather is remembered in Boston chiefly as an irrepressible humourist.
In his interesting compilation of historical
facts and personal reminiscences concerning ancient Boston, "Dealings with the
Dead," M.ʳ Lucius Manlius Sargent says :
"D.ʳ Byles has been wafted down the
stream of time, to distant ages, as it were,
upon a feather"; what he could never

have accomplished of reputation "by his
grave discourses and elaborate poetical
labours, he certainly and signally achieved
by his never-to-be-forgotten quips and
cranks and bon mots and puns and funny
sayings and comical doings."[41] "His wit,"
says Doctor Nathaniel Emmons, "bubbled
up as naturally as spring water, and his
witticisms kept Boston on a broad grin
for all of half a century. You heard them
repeated on the streets and at the most
select dinner parties. They entitled him
to a monument, because they promoted
the public health by aiding public diges-
tion." "The first story I ever heard of
Mather Byles," says M[r] Sargent, "was
related at my father's table by the Rev.
D[r] Belknap in 1797. It was upon a Saturday, and D[r] John Clarke and some other
gentlemen, among whom I well remember Major General Lincoln, ate their
salt fish there that day. I was a boy,
and I remember their mirth when after

Dᴿ Belknap had told the story I said to our minister Dᴿ Clark, near whom I was eating my apple, that I wished he were half as funny a minister as Dᴿ Byles." The reputation for wit Doctor Byles had in Boston is very well shown by Thomas Morton Jones's well-known doggerel ballad on the Boston ministers of his time which was printed in 1774. Describing with coarse humour all the Boston ministers, Chauncy, Pemberton, Eliot, Cooper, Samuel Mather, and the rest, Jones says of Doctor Byles:

> "There's punning Byles invokes our smiles,
> A man of stately parts;
> He visits folks to crack his jokes,
> Which never mend their hearts.

> "With strutting gait, and wig so great,
> He walks along the streets,
> And throws out wit, or what's like it,
> To every one he meets." [42]

From such notices as these by Doctor Byles's contemporaries or the people who lived nearer his time than we, and from the examples of the doctor's wit that have come down to us, we are obliged to admit that his humour rarely if ever rises above the plane of puns or amusing jokes or sharp repartee, but such as his humour was it seems to have kept Boston laughing for more than a generation, and his scattered puns and smart sayings that have survived to our time not one of us who has any sense of humour can help finding more or less entertaining still. While he lived people met him as Greville says people always met Sydney Smith, prepared to laugh and if need be go into fits of merriment over his puns and quips.[43] Doctor Byles could be fiercely satirical but his satire had none of the sustained dignity and apparent gravity of Swift's, he could set people laughing, but his sallies always came short of the droll fun of that prince of social humourists, himself also a clergyman, Sydney Smith. Occasionally Doctor

Byles's jokes were tinged with bitter personal feeling, and it seems more than probable that his unpopularity at the Revolution was not a little the result of cutting jibes in which he had indulged at the expense of gentlemen who in the strife between England and the Colonies had espoused the American cause. Where Doctor Byles's keen sense of humour and unusual power of wit came from it is impossible to say, he could hardly have inherited it from the serious Mathers or Cottons from whom he was descended. It was much more likely an endowment from the Byleses, but of the peculiar mental qualities of this little known English family we have no knowledge at all.

It is said that on a certain Sunday morning the learned Doctor Thomas Prince was to preach for Doctor Byles, but at the hour of service had not arrived. Glancing with perturbed mind, no doubt, at the entrance to the pulpit from time to time, the doctor began the service. But Doctor Prince, who had possibly entirely forgotten the appointment, failed to come, and Doctor Byles was obliged to preach himself. The text he announced, it is said, was "Put not your trust in princes !"

The drawings for King's Chapel presented by the architect, Peter Harrison of Newport, Rhode Island, and finally accepted, showed two tiers of windows, the lower windows not much more than half the size of the upper; when Doctor Byles saw the drawings he exclaimed, referring to the lower tier of windows: "I have heard of the canons of the Church, but I never saw the port-holes before." [44]

In 1773, the *Massachusetts Gazette* informs us, the town authorities purchased for Boston from England two or three hundred street lamps. The afternoon of the day they arrived a gossipy woman who had adopted so-called "New Light" opinions, and was gifted with a disagreeable whining voice, called on Doctor Byles. Her conversation irritated and bored the doctor and at last in desperation he said: "Have you heard the news?" "No, what news, Doctor Byles?" she asked eagerly. "Why, Madam," said the parson, "three hundred new lights have this morning arrived from London, and the selectmen have wisely ordered them put in irons." "You don't say so!" said the woman, whereupon she hurried away to see who else had heard the distressing news.[45]

A gentleman whom Doctor Byles knew very kindly sent the doctor a barrel of fine oysters. Meeting the donor's wife on the street an hour or two after the oysters came, Doctor Byles said to her: "Madam, your husband has treated me this morning in a most Billingsgate manner!" and so left her. The woman, who was of a nervous temperament, went home in distress, and when her husband came to dinner told him what Doctor Byles had said. The man, it is recorded, was so annoyed at the doctor's folly that he promptly cut his acquaintance.

A poor chap in agony with the toothache asked Doctor Byles where he should go to have his tooth drawn. The Doctor directed him to a certain lonely house on the southwest side of Beacon Hill, where he told him he would find a person who would "draw it." The man went, and found, not a dentist, but John Singleton Copley, the painter. "This is a poor joke for Doctor Byles," said Copley. "I do not think my drawing your tooth would ease the pain very much."

A candidate for local fame once announced to the public that he would fly from the steeple of the North Church. He had already mounted the steeple, and was clapping his artificial wings to the delight of the crowd below, when Doctor Byles happened along. "What has this

crowd gathered for?" said the reverend
wit. "We have come, sir," said some one,
"to see a man fly." "Poh! Poh!" said
the doctor moving away, "I have seen a
horse fly."

One day a parishioner called and found
the minister diligently nailing list on
his doors to keep the cold out. The
parishioner humorously said: "The wind
bloweth where it listeth, Doctor Byles."
"Yes," answered the doctor quickly, "and
man listeth wheresoever the wind bloweth."

A certain M͏ʳ Thomas Hill had a dis-
tillery "at the corner of Essex and South
Streets, not far from where Doctor Bel-
knap's house stood, in Lincoln Street."
One day Doctor Byles saw Hill in the
Street and asked him, probably much to
the man's surprise: "Do you still?"
"That is my business," said the distiller.
"Then," said the doctor, "I wish you
would come with me and still my wife."
What had happened to disturb the serenity

of the Byles household, or whether this incident occurred in the time of the first or the second Mʳˢ Byles we are not informed.

One night after Mʳˢ Rebecca Byles and her daughters had gone to bed they were awakened by the doctor's calling loudly: "Thieves! Thieves!" Hastily springing from their beds the women rushed to Doctor Byles's study, but found the doctor calmly writing or reading at his desk. "Where? Where?" asked the women excitedly. "There!" said the doctor, pointing quietly to the candles. Another very cold night the Miss Byleses were roused from their comfortable beds by their father calling to them to get up. When they came to his study he said: "I merely wanted to know whether you lay warm in bed."

The Byles servant at one time was a very stupid and literal Irish girl, probably not long from the Emerald Isle. One day with a look of affright and in apparent agitation Doctor Byles said to her: "Go upstairs and tell your mistress that Doctor Byles has put an end to himself." The girl ran hurriedly to M.ʳˢ Byles and in a terrified voice gave the doctor's message. To the study quickly came M.ʳˢ Byles and her daughters. The vision that greeted them was of the reverend gentleman waltzing about the room with part of a cow's tail he had somewhere picked up tied to his coat behind.

One morning when M.ʳˢ Byles was ironing, some women visitors to the doctor were announced. M.ʳˢ Byles did not wish to be seen at the ironing table and allowed herself to be pushed by her husband into a closet. After a little general conversation the callers expressed a wish to see the doctor's curiosities. The parson took them about the house and finally came to the closet. "My greatest curiosity I have kept till the last," he said, then opening the door he presented to them his greatly embarrassed wife.

The road opposite the Byles house for several seasons was almost impassable in wet weather because of the deep, soft mud. Doctor Byles repeatedly complained to the selectmen of the nuisance and asked to have the road mended, but without avail. One day he looked out and saw two of the city fathers standing in the mud trying to extricate from its depths the wheels of the chaise in which they had been driving. Going out of his house Doctor Byles bowed respectfully to the selectmen and said: "Gentlemen, I have frequently represented that slough to you as a nuisance, but hitherto without any result, I am glad to see you stirring in the matter at last."

One Fast Day Doctor Byles and some brother minister out of town were to exchange pulpits. On the appointed morning both ministers started on horseback,

K

one away from the town, the other towards
it. When they came within sight of each
other Doctor Byles spurred his horse into
a gallop and passed the country minister
at full speed. "Why so fast, brother
Byles?" called out the rural parson,
halting. Looking back over his shoulder
Doctor Byles answered: "It's fast day!"

We have seen how close the friendship
between Doctor Byles and Governor Belcher was. A further illustration of this
is to be found in a story told by Doctor
Jeremy Belknap, which appears in a manuscript in Belknap's handwriting, in the
library of the Massachusetts Historical
Society, and more briefly in print in the
Massachusetts Historical Society's Collections.[46] The story shows that if Doctor
Byles could indulge in humour at the
expense of others and occasionally play
unwelcome practical jokes, in spite of
gubernatorial dignity Governor Belcher
could do the same. At some time during

his governorship of Massachusetts, M⸢ꞏ⸣
Belcher undertook a voyage to the east-
ward (it is said to Nova Scotia) to "treat"
with the Indians. The governor asked
Doctor Byles to go with him, but the
minister felt obliged to refuse. Governor
Belcher wanted his friend's company and
determined to have it, so he got the chaplain at Castle William, in the harbour, to
exchange pulpits with Doctor Byles on
the following Sunday, on the afternoon
of which day he had arranged to start.
The Governor was going in the war-ship
Scarborough, Captain Durell, and on Sunday morning he had the ship anchor near
the castle. In the afternoon he invited
Doctor Byles to come aboard to drink tea,
and while Byles was there the captain,
as directed, weighed anchor, and the minister was obliged to take the voyage.
But the story does not end here. When
another Sunday came, the weather having
been stormy, Doctor Byles found himself

still at sea. Of course he must have religious service on board and he prepared to do so. Having taken two sermons with him to Castle William he was well equipped for preaching, but nobody on board had a hymn-book. Accordingly, the minister himself wrote a hymn, and it is one that has great dignity, shows a fine imagination, and is indeed quite above mediocrity.

"Great God! Thy works our wonder raise,
To Thee our swelling notes belong;
While skies and winds and rocks and seas
Around shall echo to our song.

"Thy power produced this mighty frame,
Aloud to Thee the tempests roar;
Or softer breezes tune Thy name
Gently along the Shelly shore.

"Round Thee the scaly nation roves,
Thy opening hand their joys bestow;
Through all the blushing coral groves,
These silent gay retreats below.

"See the broad sun forsake the skies,
  Glow on the waves, and downward slide;
Anon ! heaven opens all its eyes,
  And starbeams tremble in the tide.

"Each various scene, or day or night,
  Lord, points to Thee our ravish'd soul;
Thy glories fix our whole delight,
  So the touch'd needle courts the pole."

That the composition of this fine hymn
of the sea should have exposed Doctor
Byles to subsequent satire seems at least
unfair, but as London in the eighteenth
century had fierce rivalries that led literary men into coarse satirical rhyming
against each other, so Boston had its
doggerel rhymesters who occasionally did
what they could to turn into ridicule the
literary compositions and smirch if they
were able the reputations of other writers
whom they disliked. As a humourist Doctor Byles had one acknowledged rival in
Boston, who was almost exactly of his
own age, and who had graduated at Har-

vard a year later than he, a merchant (the doctor says "distiller") named Joseph Green. Although not a professional man, Green too dabbled a good deal in literature, writing in the newspapers and occasionally venturing into print in a pamphlet. His writing was in both prose and verse, his poetry being frequently humorous and always readable because of the smoothness with which his numbers flowed. Towards Doctor Byles he evidently had none too amiable a feeling and he was never averse to holding the minister of Hollis Street up to ridicule by parodying his poetry and in other conspicuous ways. It is said that the doctor's friend Governor Belcher was also frequently a target for Green's shots, and that this official stood a good deal in awe of Green.[47] When the fact of Doctor Byles's writing the hymn at sea became currently known in Boston, Green saw fit to ridicule both the episode

and the hymn itself. The hymn, as we
have seen, was somewhat minutely descriptive, and this feature of it especially
came in for Green's satire. In order to
treat properly with the Indians Governor
Belcher was supposed to have taken with
him on the voyage a goodly quantity of
rum, and this fact also Green does not
fail to make trenchant allusion to in his
parody. The satire reads:

"In David's Psalms an oversight
  Byles found one morning o'er his tea.
Alas, why did not David write
  A proper psalm to sing at sea?

"Awhile he paused and stroked his Muse,[48]
  Then, taking up his tuneful pen,
Wrote a few stanzas for the use
  Of his seafaring brethren.

"The task perform'd, the Bard content,
  Well chosen was each flowing word;
On a short voyage himself he went,
  To hear it read and sung on board.

"What extasies of joy appear,
  What pleasures and unknown delights
Thrilled the vain poet's soul to hear
  Others repeat the things he writes.

"Most aged Christians do aver,
  Their credit sure we may rely on,
In former times, that after prayer
  They used to sing a song of Zion;

"Our modern parson, having pray'd,
  Unless loud fame our faith beguiles,
Sat down, took out his book, and said,
  'Let's sing a song of Mather Byles.'

"As soon as he began to read,
  Their heads the assembly downward hung,
But he with boldness did proceed,
  And thus he read, and thus they sung, —

"THE 151st PSALM

"With vast amazement we survey
  The wonders of the deep,
Where mackrel swim, and porpoise play,
  And crabs and lobsters creep.

"Fish of all kinds inhabit there,
  And throng the dark abode;

There haddick, hake, and flounders are,
And eels and perch and cod.

"From raging winds and tempests free,
So smooth that as you pass,
The shining surface seems to be
A piece of Bristol glass.

"But when the winds tempestuous rise,
And foaming billows swell,
The vessel mounts above the skies,
Then lower sinks than hell.

"Our brains the tottering motion feel,
And quickly we become
Giddy as new-dropt calves, and reel
Like Indians drunk with rum.

"What praises then are due that we
Thus far have safely got,
Amariscoggin tribe to see,
And tribe of Penobscot."

Before long Doctor Byles retorted on
Green with a parody on Green's parody,
which Doctor Belknap says distinctly
turned the laugh on Green. Doctor
Byles's parody in one form (for there is

another slightly different version) is as follows :

> "In Byles's hymns an oversight
> Green spy'd as once he smok'd his Chunk ;
> Alas ! the Byles should never write
> A song to sing when folks are drunk.

[Doctor Belknap in a letter to Ebenezer Hazard quotes the stanza from memory thus :

> "In Byles's hymns an oversight
> Green spy'd one evening o'er his junk ;
> Alas ! why did not Byles indite
> A song to sing when folks are drunk."]

> "Thus in the chimney, on his block,
> Ambition fir'd the 'stiller's pate,
> He summoned all his little stock,
> The poet's volume to complete.

> "Long paus'd the lout, and scratch'd his skull,
> Then took his chalk (he own'd no pen),
> And scrawl'd some doggrel, for the whole
> Of his flip-drinking brethren.

> "The task perform'd — not to content —
> Ill chosen was each Grub-street word ;

Strait to the tavern club he went,
To hear it bellow'd round the board.

"Unknown delights his ears explore,
Inur'd to midnight caterwauls,
To hear his hoarse companions roar,
The horrid thing his dulness scrawls.

"The club, if fame we may rely on,
Conven'd, to hear the drunken catch,
At the three horse-shoes or red lion —
Tippling began the night's debauch.

"The little 'stiller took the pint
Still fraught with flip and songs obscene,
And, after a long stutt'ring, meant
To sing a song of Josy Green.

"Soon as with stam'ring tongue, to read
The drunken ballad, he began,
The club from clam'ring strait recede,
To hear him roar the thing alone.

"Song

"With vast amazement we survey
The can so broad, so broad, so deep,
Where punch succeeds to strong gangree,
Both to delightful flip.

"Drink of all smacks, inhabit here,
And throng the dark abode;
Here's rum, and sugar, and small beer,
In a continual flood.

"From cruel thoughts and conscience free,
From dram to dram we pass;
Our cheeks, like apples, ruddy be;
Our eyeballs look like glass.

"At once, like furies, up we rise,
Our raging passions swell;
We hurl the bottle to the skies,
But why we cannot tell.

"Our brains a tott'ring motion feel,
And quickly we become
Sick, as with negro steaks, and reel
Like Indians drunk with rum.

"Thus lost in deep tranquillity,
We sit, supine and sot,
Till we two moons distinctly see —
Come give us 'tother pot."

The phrase "negro steaks," in the last
stanza but one of this parody, is an allusion
to an unsavoury story at that time current

in Boston that on one occasion some practical joker had imposed steaks cut from a dead negro, instead of beef, on the convivial club to which Green belonged.[49]

At some period in his ministerial career Doctor Byles had his study painted brown. In explanation of the rather dull colour he is said to have told people that he wanted to be able on occasion to say he was in "a brown study." On a certain day he went, perhaps somewhat reluctantly, to see a parishioner who was convalescing from smallpox. As he entered the patient's room he piously uttered what the man took to be the familiar ecclesiastical salutation, *"Pax te cum!"* Doctor Byles's actual salutation, however, was, "Pox take 'em!"

CHAPTER VIII

Dismissal from His Church

THROUGHOUT New England from the earliest times, even after the government had ceased to be strictly a theocracy, church and state were so closely united that the meeting-houses were the chief places where the fires of independence in communities were kept aflame. When the war of the Revolution was in its early stages, of the various religious meeting-houses of Boston besides the Anglican churches, there was probably only the Hollis Street Church where more or less fierce denunciations of England were not heard from the pulpits and where the congregations were not strongly urged to resistance against her oppressions. The Old South Church, as is well known, was

the scene of some of the most stirring
events of the struggle, and when the siege
of Boston began, its minister like all the
other Congregational ministers of the town
with the exception of Doctor Andrew
Eliot of the New North Church, Doctor
Samuel Mather, and Doctor Mather Byles,
at once took refuge, with a large part of
their parishioners, in the country near.
Of these ministers of Boston, and indeed
of the whole body of Congregational ministers in New England, Doctor Byles alone
sympathized with the crown. In the
"Memorial History of Boston" the writer
on the Boston "Pulpit of the Revolution"
says: Doctor Byles "tried, with un-
doubted sincerity, to avoid politics in
the pulpit, but his opinions were too
notorious, and his sharp tongue was too
free, to make his position long an agreeable one either to his people or to himself." Mr Ephraim Eliot in his historical
notices of the New North Church says that

Doctor Andrew Eliot's remaining in town
during the siege was enforced probably by
the selectmen, so that Congregational worship should be maintained; Doctor Byles,
he says, "being in the Tory interest was
neglected by most of the inhabitants,
although he performed service for some time
in one of the central meeting-houses."

That Doctor Byles persistently refused
to preach on political subjects, when all
the other ministers of his denomination
were doing so, seems to have produced
great dissatisfaction among his people.
In answer to their queries as to why he
avoided politics in his sermons he is reported to have sententiously said: "I
have thrown up four breastworks, behind
which I have entrenched myself, neither
of which can be forced.   In the first place,
I do not understand politics; in the second
place, you all do, every man and mother's
son of you; in the third place, you have
politics all the week, — pray let one day

out of seven be devoted to religion; and in the fourth place, I am engaged in a work of infinitely greater importance. Give me any subject to preach upon of more consequence than the truths I bring to you, and I will preach upon it the next Sabbath." For the unique position Doctor Byles held among his brethren of the Congregational clergy, in the great political struggle of the country through which he lived, it is on the whole not difficult to find the reasons. No Puritan minister in New England in his time, probably, had lived in so close friendly relations with the leading government officials and their families as he, and his sympathies socially were profoundly with the more conservative class. In the second place he was a poet and the vulgar clash of political parties and the details of political administration, as with many such men, were uncongenial to him, and he preferred as much as possible to let them alone.

L

So far as we know, Doctor Byles has nowhere left on record in any detail his views on the several questions that were so fiercely in dispute in the Revolutionary struggle, but he undoubtedly had views on them all, and at times expressed them, and his views were the common ones of the Tory party, with whom his sympathies were. "In March, 1770," says his friend Doctor Nathaniel Emmons, "I stood with Parson Byles on the corner of what are now School and Washington streets and watched the funeral procession of Crispus Attucks, that half Indian, half negro, and altogether rowdy, who should have been strangled long before he was born. There were all of three thousand in the procession, the most of them drawn from the slums of Boston; and as they went by the Parson turned to me and said — 'They call me a brainless Tory; but tell me, my young friend, which is better, to be ruled by one tyrant three thousand miles away, or by three thousand tyrants not a mile away?'" Doctor Emmons is further quoted as saying to the friend to whom he related this incident: [50] "I tell you, my boy, there was just as much humbug in politics seventy years ago as there is to-day; and throwing out Sam and John Adams and John Hancock, and some few other leaders, the majority of our New England patriots were a sorry set."

In the twenty-seventh volume of the New England Historical and Genealogical Register, in a note on the May family of Boston a writer says: "Doctor Byles, as is well known, was a steady opponent of the patriotic movement, of which Boston was the headquarters, and in all ways strove to ridicule it and its principal supporters. As he gave very free expression to his feelings, his opponents, of course, were not backward in their censures of him." The statement that

while Byles refused to discuss politics
in the pulpit he gave free rein to his powers
of sarcasm in opposition to the Patriot
cause is undoubtedly true, for while one
of his deacons, Mr. Benjamin Church,
sympathized with the Tories and upheld
his minister, most of the Hollis Street
congregation were extremely bitter against
him, the May family, at least, withdrawing
from the Hollis Street Church and uniting
with the Old South. When the royal
troops invested Boston most of Doctor
Byles's congregation that could get away
hurried out of the town, but the doctor
and his family stayed, and his staying was
one of the charges brought against him
when his congregation at last returned.

In this day of clear judgment on the
issues at stake in the Revolution, the
bitterness Doctor Byles felt towards the
Patriots in Boston is not hard to explain.
Like his friend Copley he had no doubt
long foreseen that unless England changed

her policy towards the colonies, a revolt
was inevitable, but when the crisis came
he saw so much fanaticism mingled with
the true spirit of independence that like
many another man of patriotic but conservative views he was disgusted with
the outbreaks of feeling he witnessed and
contemptuous of the methods by which
many of his fellow-citizens sought to
redress their wrongs. We have spoken
of his probable intimacy with Earl Percy,
"I am sorry to say," wrote Percy to his
father, in 1774, "that no body of men in
this Province are so extremely injurious
to the peace and tranquillity of it as the
clergy. They preach up sedition openly
from their pulpits. Nay, some of them
have gone so far as absolutely to refuse
the sacrament to the communicants till
they have signed a paper of the most
seditious kind, which they have denomi-
nated the Solemn League and Covenant."
To Henry Reveley, Esq., of Peckham,

Surrey, he writes: "The people here are a set of sly, artful, hypocritical rascals, cruel and cowards. I must own I cannot but despise them completely." "This day, five years are completed," writes Judge Samuel Curwen in his journal in 1780, "since I abandoned my house, estate, and effects and friends. God only knows whether I shall ever be restored to them, or they to me. Party rage, like jealousy and superstition is cruel as the grave; that moderation is a crime, . . . many good virtuous, and peaceable persons now suffering banishment from America are the wretched proofs and instances." "Would to God," he earlier writes, "this ill-judged, unnatural quarrel were ended."

While the British were in possession of the town Doctor Byles and his family were evidently on terms of close friendship with the leading commanders of the troops, and Mr Harold Murdock is probably

quite right in imagining Doctor Byles
to have been an occasional guest at Earl
Percy's dinner table, in the house this
charming young nobleman had rented at
the head of Winter Street, on the edge of
the Common. But Byles's intimacy with
British officers did not prevent the quarter-
ing of troops in the Hollis Street meeting-
house, as in the Old South and the Brattle
Street Churches, and when Doctor Byles's
congregation came back they found to
their great indignation the pews taken
down and stored in the gallery, to be used
as fuel should necessity require, a box
stove set up in the church, the pipe of
which went perpendicularly through the
roof, and the floor still littered with straw,
which had no doubt served the soldiers
as beds. Collecting their forces, the
leaders of the congregation accordingly
resolved without further delay to rid themselves of their unpatriotic pastor, whose
voice they were stoutly resolved never

to hear in their pulpit again. The regular
way of dismissing him would have been
to call an advisory council of sister
churches to review his conduct and counsel the church how to act. But instead
of doing this they took matters promptly
into their own hands and prepared to deal
with the minister by themselves.

In pursuance of this resolve, they gave
public notice that on the 9th of August
(1776) the church would meet Doctor
Byles and give him a chance to answer
the charges they had to prefer against
him. When the day came the male members of the church seated themselves in
one of the galleries, and waited for the
doctor to appear. Presently he entered,
dressed in gown and bands, on his head
a full bush wig that had been recently
powdered, surmounted by a large three-
cornered hat. With due solemnity of
bearing and with a long and measured
tread Byles walked to the pulpit and

1776. August 9th This Church haveing been for Some
Time driven (by the Cruel hand of Brittan)
from their habitations, and their house of
Worship been Turned into a Barrack by
their Enemies — have now by the grate
goodness of God an opportunity to visit
their habitations — This day assem=
=bled in the Meetinghouse to Consider the
Conduct of the Revd Dor Byles our pastor
who Remaind in the Town durring the time
of its being in Possesion of the Enemy and
to our grate greif appears to have Joined
our them against the Liberties of
our Country — this being a matter of
grate Importance and we being few in
Number. It was moved that the Church
Should Unite with the Congregation In the
Consideration & determination of this
Matter. which being put Pasd in the
affirmative unanimously and the Congregation
unanimously Agreed to the Proposal —

ascended the stairs. Hanging his hat on a peg, he seated himself, and after a few moments silence, "with a portentous air" turned towards the gallery where his accusers sat. Looking at them sternly he called out: "If ye have aught to communicate, say on!" After a moment of terrible stillness, a small, weak-voiced deacon arose, and unfolding a paper began feebly to read. "The church of Christ in Hollis Street" — he said. "Louder!" cried the angry Doctor Byles. Again the little deacon, trying to raise his voice, began: "The church of Christ in Hollis Street" — But again the doctor's stentorian voice thundered out "Louder!" A third time the deacon essayed to read, when once more he was interrupted with "Louder! Louder, I say!" The deacon now, trembling at the minister's wrath, strained his voice to the utmost and read the specifications of unministerial and unpatriotic conduct on the doctor's part which he and his fellow-members had laboriously drawn up. When the third or fourth charge had been read Doctor Byles rose and shouted at the top of his voice: "'Tis false! 'Tis false! 'Tis false! and the Church of Christ in Hollis Street knows that 'tis false!" whereupon he seized his hat, planted it firmly on his head, and in fierce indignation dramatically moved out of the church, never while he lived to enter its doors again.

The specific charges made against Doctor Byles by his people were, that he had stayed in town during the siege; that he had "pray'd in publick that America might submitt to Grate Brittain, or words to the same purpose"; that he "associated and spent a considerable part of his time with the officers of the British army, having them frequently at his house and lending them his glasses for the purpose of seeing the works erecting out of town for our Defense"; that he treated the public calamity with "a grate degree of liteness and Indifference, saying when his townspeople left their houses that a better sort of people would take their place, or words to that purpose"; and that "he frequently met on Lord's days, before and after service, with a number of our Inveterate Enemies, at a certain place in King Street called Tory Hall." One week later than the doctor's dramatic arraignment in the meeting-house the church again met and voted "that the Rev.ᵈ Doctor Mather Byles, having by his conduct put an end to his usefulness as a Publick preacher amongst us, Be and hereby is, dismissed from his Pastoral charge." ⁵¹

Of the general truth of these accusations of the church against Doctor Byles we suppose there can be no doubt. Precisely what his feelings were, or indeed the feelings of many of his fellow Tories, as they witnessed for years previous to the Revolution the growing friction between the royal governors and the general court, the contest of the writs of assistance, the riotous outbursts against the Stamp Act, the throwing of the tea into the harbour, the fights along the road between Concord and Lexington, the battle of Bunker Hill, Washington's taking command of the army at Cambridge and his memorable seizure of Dorchester Heights, we are left to imagine, but while he was far too intelligent and patriotic not to have been stirred by his country's grievances, Byles no doubt, with many others, felt that it was a far smaller evil to submit temporarily to British oppression, caused by the stupid obstinacy and want of statesmanlike knowledge of ministers, than violently to cast off allegiance to the British flag, and whatever influence he had as a clergyman and a private gentleman he had naturally thrown wholly on the unpopular side. That the British officers of highest

rank in command of the forces were frequently entertained at his house during
the siege was undoubtedly true, it is even
said that on this account, and because
of the detestation in which he was generally held for his political principles, the
blinds in his house had to be kept tightly
closed in the evenings during the latter
part of the siege, lest the lights shining
out should make the house a target for
unfriendly shots from the soldiers en-
camped on Dorchester Heights.

Although the bitterest feeling against
Doctor Byles existed in the minds of his
fellow-ministers when they returned to
their churches, it is evident that some of
them entirely disapproved of the course
the Hollis Street Church had taken in not
seeking advice from other churches in
dissolving the relations between them and
their pastor. "It was the greatest in-
jury to the ministry that ever was done
when this church proceeded to dismiss

D: Byles without any kind of advice from an Ecclesiastical Council," writes young Rev. John Eliot from Boston to his friend Rev. Jeremy Belknap at Dover, June 17th, 1777. A little earlier M: Eliot says: "D: Byles's church is supplied by Mr. Bradford, a young gentleman, a friend of mine, a new beginner. The Doctor struts about town in the luxuriance of his self-sufficiency, looking as if he despised all mankind. He never attends any meeting. How he doth for a maintenance, nobody knows besides him, and the only account he can give us is, 'That he doubles and trebles his money.' He is a virulent Tory, and destitute of all prudence. . . . Notwithstanding I despise D: Byles as much as a man can hold another, yet I think y⁰ proceedings of that church with him were irregular and unwarrantable, and hath held up a precedent for a practise that will cause y⁰ ruin of our ecclesiastical constitution, weaken y⁰ hands of y⁰ ministry, and lay such discouragement before candidates as will prevent their settling, and in a few years the harvest must be almost destitute of labourers. When the church at Bolton made this innovation D.r Chauncy was so angry that he would have refused holding communion with the members; yet now he justifies and was the cause of this church at Boston proceeding in the way they have done. He says, 'Byles is not fit for a preacher.' So say I, but I would have had a Council, and I am certain any Council would have given him his quietus." [52]

The reason given by M.r Ephraim Eliot for Doctor Byles's summary dismissal from his pastorate is that he not only had offended his people by his Tory principles, but had lost their respect by indulging "in a natural vein of low wit and ridiculous punning." [53] If the latter charge is true we must accept it largely on M.r Eliot's statement: we believe it has no

explicit confirmation in any other published writing. Of the abrupt termination of Doctor Byles's ministry, Rev.
George Leonard Chaney, a late pastor of
the Hollis Street Church says: "Although
ordinarily D: Byles's pastorate would
have lasted till his death, at that day
politics and religion were so much one
that unfaithfulness to civil liberty was
regarded by these patriots as an unpar-
donable offence against the Church. It
was on this ground that the tie between
pastor and people was broken, a tie which
at that time was as binding as that which
wedded man and wife."

CHAPTER IX

TRIAL BEFORE THE TOWN

AFTER his dismissal from his pastorate a further trial and condemnation for his Tory principles awaited Doctor Byles from the Boston civil authorities. In the Records of the Committee of Correspondence and Safety of August, 1776, we find: "Information having been given this Committee of a number of Persons who had heard Doctor Byles express himself very unfriendly to this Country, M̲r Thomas was directed to require their attendance. A number of Persons appeared and were examined as to what they knew relative to Doctor Byles." In a meeting held on the 17ᵗʰ of May, 1777, the Boston selectmen in pursuance of a law that had lately been passed presented a list of names of persons belonging to the town who had been endeavouring, as it was charged, "since the 19th of April, 1775, to counter-act the united struggles of this and the neighbouring state," and of these offend-ing names Doctor Byles's stood second. At a special Sessions of the Peace held on the second of June, Byles was tried and convicted of disloyalty to the state and was ordered to be confined on board a guard ship or otherwise secured, until he could be sent either to the West Indies or to Europe. In the Massachusetts His-torical Society Collections is printed an extract from the *Boston Gazette* of June 9, 1777,[54] which says: "At the special Ses-sions of the Peace held here on Monday last came on the trial of Mather Byles, late minister of the Gospel in this town, charged with being an enemy to the United States; when after a fair and candid ex-amination of evidence the jury returned their verdict, that he, Mather Byles, is and has been since the 19th of April, 1775, inimically disposed towards this and the other United States, and that his residence in this State is dangerous to the public peace and safety. He was then delivered into the custody of a proper officer, who conducted him to the Honourable the Board of War, there to be dealt with agreeable to a late act of this State, for such persons made and provided."

William Tudor in his "Life of James Otis" says of Doctor Byles's trial: "On being brought before the Board of War he was treated with respect, and he was ordered to be confined to his own house for a short time." "As there seems to have been nothing absolutely treasonable in his conduct," he rather naïvely proceeds, "it may be doubted whether he would have experienced any inconvenience on account of his political sentiments if he had not provoked enmity in other ways. He possessed in a remarkable degree a ready and powerful wit, a quality which commonly excites more envy than good will, and unless accompanied with great discretion is often an unfortunate gift. He sometimes exerted this talent where good nature would have refrained, and left a lasting sting by a transient jest." In a volume of manuscript records in the Massachusetts State Archives pertaining to the Royalists in the Revolution, is to be found the following warrant issued by the Court of Sessions to the sheriff for Doctor Byles's arrest and transportation: "Whereas Mather Byles of Boston in s^d county, clerk, stands convicted at Boston afores^d on the second Day of June A.D. 1777 as a person who hath been from the nineteenth day of April A.D. 1775, & now is so inimically disposed towards this & the other United States of America that his further residence in this State is dangerous to the public peace and safety, You are therefore in the name of the gov-

ernment & people of Mass.ª Bay in New
England hereby directed immediately to
deliver the s.ᵈ Mather to the board of war
of the State to be by them put on board
a guard ship or otherwise secured until
they can transport s.ᵈ Mather Byles off
the continent to some part of the West
Indies or Europe agreeable to a late law
of s.ᵈ State. Given under our hands and
seals at Boston afores.ᵈ the second day of
June in the year of the Lord 1777.

JOHN HILL
SAML. PEMBERTON
JOSEPH GREENLEAF
JOSEPH GARDNER

Justices of s.ᵈ Court

The warrant is endorsed on the back:
"Warrant to deliver Mather Byles to the
Board of War June 2.ᵈ 1777."

Under date of June 18, 1777, the Rev.
Doctor Ezra Stiles in his diary says:
"The Rev.ᵈ M.ʳ Clark, Episc° Minister
in Dedham, was last week adjudged by a
Jury an enemy to his Country, and sent

on board the Guard Ship at Boston. So one Episc° and one Presb. Minister (Dr. Byles) formally tried and condemned accord to act of Mass. Assembly." [55]

What influence may have prevented the Boston authorities' carrying out the rigorous sentence they had imposed on Doctor Byles we are nowhere certainly told. It has been said in print that the doctor flatly told the selectmen that he would not leave the town, it has also been stated that in their final dealing with the old minister the authorities considered his age, which at this time was a little over seventy. It may be, even, though it hardly seems likely, that some one or more of the other Boston ministers interceded to have his sentence remitted, at any rate he was not placed on the guard ship but was confined to his own house, before which a sentinel was placed to prevent his being visited by or having communication with any friends he might still have in the town. For probably two or three months, with a short interval during which the sentinel was removed, the farce of guarding the old Tory was kept up, but at last his absurd imprisonment came to an end, and he was allowed once more freely to go about the town.

In July, 1778, while Doctor Byles was imprisoned in his house the Rev. Jacob Bailey, an Episcopal clergyman, well known to us as "the frontier missionary," came from Pownalborough, Maine, to Boston, on business, and was permitted to visit the old Royalist. Under date of July 23ᵈ Mʳ Bailey writes in his diary: "After breakfast went to visit the famous Dʳ Byles, who was detained a prisoner in his own house. He received me, according to his manner, with great freedom, and entertained me with a variety of puns. He was mightly pleased with the letters I brought him from his son and granddaughter, and instructed his daughters, a

couple of fine young ladies, to read them.[56]
I observed that he had a large collection
of curiosities, and the best library I had
seen in this country. He is a gentleman
of learning and great imagination, has an
uncommon share of pride, and though
agreeable when discoursing upon any subject, yet the perpetual reaching after puns
renders his ordinary conversation rather
distasteful to persons of elegance and
refinement. He gave me a circumstantial
account of his trial when condemned for
transportation. He carefully preserved his
talent for punning through the whole.
I recollect one instance: when he was
conducted into the apartment where his
judges sat with great solemnity, who desired him to sit by the fire, as the weather
was cold: 'Gentlemen,' said he, 'when I
came among you I expected persecution,
but I could not think you would have
offered me the fire so suddenly.' After
looking at several fine prospects, and hear-

ing two or three tunes on the organ by one of his daughters, I took my leave, with an invitation and promise to renew my visit."

Of the doctor's trial and his conduct throughout the ordeal, and of the justice of the verdict given against him, young John Eliot, not yet ordained, with characteristic bitterness against the old minister, and with the cocksureness of youth writes to Jeremy Belknap: "I will acquaint a little about our Bostonian court. The first called to the bar was the magnificent Doctor. He had on his large whig [sic], long band, a black coat, &c. He appeared without counsel, and upon the nomination of the jury he objected to one Fallas, commonly called Fellows, because he said he would not be tried by *fellows*. The evidence was much more in favour of him than against him. All that could be proved was that he is a silly, impertinent, childish *person;* I should say inconsistent, if his whole conduct did not manifest him to be one consistent lump of absurdity. . . . It was to the very great surprise of every one present, as well as to the whole town, that he should be bro't in guilty. His general character has been so despicable that he seems to have no friends to pity him, tho all allow upon such evidence he o't not be condemned. The women all proclaim a judgment from Heaven as a punishment for his ill treatment of his wives. Vengeance has at length overtaken him, they say, and his present sufferings will now bring him to reflection, and he will now find that a Righteous Being taketh notice of all unrighteousness among men, and at proper times humbles the most haughty and self-sufficient. The Doctor is still confined to his house, deprived of visitors, to be removed at the pleasure of the Board of War. How are the mighty fallen !" [57]

From Miss Catherine Byles, the doctor's youngest daughter, we have an in-

teresting account, written on the thirteenth
of October, 1778, of the trial of her father
by the church and the town authorities.
Miss Byles writes: "Upon the first opening of the town [after the evacuation], the
people among whom my father had offi-
ciated for forty-three years had an irregular
meeting and desired his attendance; when
a charge of his attachment to government
was read, of which, as he never could obtain a copy, I am unable to give an exact
account. Among others were included his
friendly disposition to the British troops,
particularly his entertaining them at our
house, indulging them with his telescope,
&c., his prayers for the King, and for
the preservation of the town during the
siege. Some time after this a few lines
were sent him, informing him that six
weeks before (without so much as the
advice of any Council) he had been dismissed from his pastoral charge. Thus
they left him without any support, or so

much as paying his arrears, so that from the 19th of April, 1775, to this day he has received no assistance from them. They then repaired the church, which had been occupied as a barrack for the British army, and made choice of a new pastor. In May, 1777, at a town-meeting he was mentioned as a person inimical to America; a warrant was served and bonds given for his appearance the 2nd of June, for a trial, when as they expressed it, 'after a candid and impartial examination,' he was brought in Guilty, confined to his house and land, and a guard placed to prevent the visits of his friends; and (except the removal of the guard, which was in about two months) in this confinement has he remained ever since; and had it not been for the generous assistance of his benevolent friends he must inevitably have suffered." [58]

In addition to the somewhat contemptuous witticisms in the presence of his judges in which Doctor Byles is re-

ported by M.ʳ Bailey and M.ʳ Eliot to
have indulged, we have the following
stories, handed down by tradition, of his
humour while he was suffering political
disgrace. In his trial before the justices
of the peace a certain Ebenezer ——,
commonly known as "Ebby" was summoned to give evidence. The man was
probably giving his testimony in too low
a tone for the doctor to hear, when suddenly the old wit leaning forward, with
his hand to his ear called out: "What
does that Ebby-dunce say?" "Who is
that man in uniform before your house?"
once queried some one of the doctor
while he was being guarded by a sentinel.
"O," said Doctor Byles quickly, "that
is my observe-a-Tory!" One warm day
during his imprisonment, Byles wanted
some cool water and begged the sentinel
to go to the well and get some for him.
At first the soldier, a simple fellow, refused, but on the doctor's telling him

that he himself would keep guard, the man consented to go. Doctor Byles then taking the man's musket put it on his own shoulder, and with a true military air paced up and down before his door till the soldier returned. As we have said, Doctor Byles's guard was for a time withdrawn, then replaced, and at last removed altogether. Alluding to this fact, the witty minister is reported to have said: "I have been guarded, re-guarded, and disregarded."

General Howe with his troops left Boston on the 17th of March, 1776, and on the 20th General Washington's troops came in over the Neck. Colonel Henry Knox, afterward General Knox, who had previously kept a fashionable book-store in Cornhill and was extremely well known to Doctor Byles, was in command of the artillery, and he had grown very stout.[59] At some point on their route through the town Doctor Byles was standing on the sidewalk watching the troops and when Knox came along he exclaimed: "I never saw an ox fatter in my life!" When Knox was told of the pun he is said to have remarked that Doctor Byles was "a damned fool."

It is recorded that once, before the Revolution, the doctor created almost a panic among the British troops by reporting that on the fourteenth of June forty thousand men would rise up in opposition to them, with the clergy at their head. Doctor Byles's meaning was that the 14th of June was to be the annual New England Fast Day, when political sermons would be generally preached and all the grievances of the colonies against England with great warmth be discussed. "We smile," says Rev. George L. Chaney, "at the possibility of finding anything formidable in a Fast-day congregation, but in that day, in this Province, it meant, in all literalness, an army of two-score thousand men, headed by their clergy, and animated with the dangerous resolution to defend their liberties." From the time of the Stamp Act, in 1765, to the period of the Revolution, says the author of "Dealings with the Dead," the cry had been repeated "in every form of phraseology" that Massachusetts' grievances should be redressed. In October, 1768, the British Government sent two Irish regiments, and a detachment of troops from Halifax to the assistance of Governor Bernard; "something short of a thousand men, in red coats, with glittering firelocks charged and bayonets fixed, marched through the town, with drums beating and fifes playing." Doctor Byles watching the new forces is reported to have said that Massachusetts had sent over to England to obtain a redress of her grievances, and that these grievances had returned "*red-dressed*." "True, Sir," said an acquaintance standing near, "but you have two d's." "To be sure, I have," quickly answered the Doctor, "I had them from Aberdeen in 1765." [60]

CHAPTER X

Social Standing. Friendships

THE place held by Mather Byles in the social life of Boston in the Provincial period was distinctly an important one. There were people in the community who disliked him, for the air of superiority he seems commonly to have worn, for the combative spirit of the Mathers, which he had inherited to a certain degree, for the sometimes far too caustic tone of his humour, and indeed, it is quite evident, for the humour itself, and we more than suspect from the preference he showed in social intercourse for men of position and influence, but there were few, we believe, who would have ventured to question his intellectual superiority, or his right in the catalogue of locally important men to

a place beside the scholarly Doctor
Thomas Prince of the Old South, Charles
Chauncy, Byles's contemporary through
all but the last year of his life, Joseph
Sewall, Jonathan Mayhew, or any others
of the most eminent preachers and writers
of Boston or the lesser New England
towns. What estimate the most critical
people of his time put on his poetry we
do not know, but his poems as a young
man in welcome of royal governors, and
the accession and death of monarchs, and
in commemoration of local men and women
who had occupied high official or social
stations in the community, must have
given him the local distinction of almost
a New England poet-laureate.

The exact social rank Doctor Byles
had in Boston to the time of the Revolution we may without much difficulty and
with a good deal of certainty make out.
By the time he reached manhood the
supremacy of the famous Mather

THOMAS PRINCE, A.M.

Quintus Ecclesiæ Australis Bostoni Novanglorum Pastor, è Collegii Harvardini
CANTABRIGIÆ Curatoribus SAMUELIS Armigeri Filius et Thomæ AM. donati Pater

Printed for & Sold by I. Buck & at ye Seellerbar in Queenstreet Boston. 1750.

dynasty under which he had been born
had passed, his grandfather Increase, "the
most powerful individual force in
America" in his day, and his stupendous
uncle Cotton, having died within less than
five years of each other, the latter in
February, 1728, but the prestige that
these eminent relatives had for so long
enjoyed was not by any means forgotten,
and Byles could not have failed in some
measure to inherit the distinction the
Mathers had earned. As the pastor for
over forty years of one of the less influential churches of Boston his ecclesiastical
position would not necessarily have entitled him to the social consideration he
was evidently given, but at the outset of
his ministry, if not earlier, he came into
confidential relations with the rich Governor Belcher, whose niece he soon married, and his friendly intercourse with
royal governors did not cease when Belcher
yielded the reins of government to Shirley,

or indeed probably until Gage's brief,
stormy rule came to an end. As the
Revolution drew on he identified himself
closely in political sympathy with the
crown officials and rich merchants and
leading lawyers, who for the most part
were Tories, and although many of these
were staunch supporters of the Anglican
Church and worshippers at King's Chapel,
his intercourse with them must necessarily
have been exceedingly friendly, and his
social separation from the less aristocratic
Patriot Congregational families of the town
correspondingly great.

The Boston of Doctor Byles's lifetime,
before the Revolution drove its acknowledged aristocracy away, was much like a
flourishing English provincial town. In
1760 it had about twenty-five thousand
inhabitants and was probably the largest,
and certainly, from the extent of its foreign commerce, the amount of capital
it had accumulated, and the fact that it

was the central point and chief city of the most compact population to be found on the American seaboard, the most important town in the new world. It had many wharves from which vessels were constantly plying to other parts of America, the West Indies, Europe, and the Orient, the most noted of these of course being Long Wharf, lined with warehouses, from which busy State Street, then King Street, led to near the centre of the town. At the head of this street was the Town House, where the government in all its branches met, and beneath which some of the well-known merchants had their stores. On the summit of Beacon Hill stood the tall beacon, on cross-timbers, resting on a stone foundation and supported by braces. The Common was a huge grassy public field, and the Mall, which led along the eastern side of this historic inclosure, from Park Street to West Street, bordered by lux-

uriant trees, the first of which were planted
between 1722 and 1729, was the fashionable promenade. On Tremont, School,
Beacon, and Washington streets were
"mansions" of considerable size and elegance, whose owners lived luxuriously,
some of them indeed in what local historians are accustomed to call "princely
style." One of the most conspicuous of
these mansions was the fine brick house
on Tremont Street built by Peter Faneuil,
the richest Bostonian of his day, who
died in 1742, shortly after having made
his gift of Faneuil Hall to the town.
There, to the time of his death, Faneuil
lived elegantly, with slaves, an abundance
of heavy plate, and a cellar stocked with
wines. At the time of the Revolution
the house was owned by John Vassall of
Cambridge, who probably lived in it in
winter, but Vassall, an aristocrat and
staunch Tory, was proscribed and banished, and the Faneuil house like his other

properties was confiscated and thereafter
was occupied by humbler folk. On Beacon
Street, a little to the westward of the
State House grounds, stood Thomas Hancock's house, one of the "noblest private
mansions" in Boston, built in 1737, which
in time passed to John Hancock, who
alone of the merchant-aristocrats of Boston, for one reason or another, did not
give his sympathy to the royal cause.
The estate that had originally belonged
to Rev. John Cotton, on Tremont Street,
a little to the north of Peter Faneuil's,
was owned at the Revolution by William
Vassall, while Richard Clarke, Copley's
father-in-law, who with Joshua Winslow,
Benjamin Faneuil, Jr., and Elisha and
Thomas Hutchinson, was a consignee of
the tea that was thrown into the harbour,
lived on School Street, a little below
where the Parker House stands now. Of
other men of prominence, William Phillips
lived in the house built by his father-in-

law, Edward Bromfield, on Beacon Street,
almost opposite the Athenæum; James
Bowdoin had a house, which almost
rivalled the Bromfield-Phillips house "in
solidity and elegance," a little to the west
of this house; Gilbert De Blois had a
house on Tremont Street, at the corner
of Bromfield Street; Judge Robert
Auchmuty, Jr., when the Revolution began lived in School Street; Jonathan
Snelling lived in Hanover Street; Harrison Gray lived probably on Washington
Street, north of State Street; while Governor Thomas Hutchinson, and before his
death Sir Charles Henry Frankland, as
is well known, lived in the extreme North
End.[61] One of Doctor Byles's intimate
friends was John Singleton Copley, whose
estate of eleven acres, the largest at the
time in Boston, lay on the southwest
side of Beacon Hill, between Beacon and
Pinckney, and Walnut and Charles streets.
His house of two stories was of wood,

and possibly not a very handsome one,
but in it he painted some of his most
noted portraits, and received visitors, clad
magnificently in a crimson velvet, gold-
laced suit, his income of three hundred
guineas a year enabling him to live in a
style befitting his position as Boston's
most eminent "court-painter."

Another warm friend of Doctor Byles
for many years was a Boston born man,
slightly older than himself, who, however,
early separated himself from the town of
his nativity, and in the great Revolutionary struggle sympathized with and cham-
pioned not the royalist party to which
Doctor Byles belonged, but the Patriots,
whose actions this ardent upholder of
British supremacy in New England cor-
dially hated and scorned. This friend of
Doctor Byles's was no less a person than
Doctor Benjamin Franklin,[62] with whom,
although his early associations in Boston
were somewhat different from Franklin's,

as a boy and young man he probably had some little acquaintance. Just how this acquaintance really started we do not know, but it is evident that it began at an early age, and that the two men throughout their whole lives, though their correspondence was infrequent, never quite lost interest in each other's affairs. In an earlier chapter we have spoken of the fierce controversy on the subject of inoculation between the Mathers and James Franklin, which occurred while Byles was a student at Harvard, and of the contemptuous way in which the militant editor and the combative young freshman spoke of each other in print. About a year later than this, for a statement he had made in his paper, the *New-England Courant*, which was regarded as a serious affront to the authorities, James Franklin was imprisoned for a month, and when he was released he was forbidden to print anything that was not first rigidly cen-

Dr. BENJAMIN FRANKLIN
From an engraving by T. B. Welch

sored by the Secretary of the Province or
some one whom he should appoint. For
some time previously Benjamin Franklin
had been his brother's apprentice, and
on James's release from prison the latter
made Benjamin nominal editor of the
paper. Although Benjamin Franklin to
this time had been merely an apprentice,
his formal assumption of the editorship
of the *Courant* must now have made him
somewhat known in the community, and
before he left Boston for Philadelphia,
which he did, however, long before his
name as editor disappeared from the
Courant, it is far from unlikely that Byles
and he had occasionally met.[63] That they
somehow became early acquainted is shown
by an interesting correspondence between
them that from various sources we have
recently been able to gather up. From
Benjamin Franklin's obscure editorship of
the *Courant*, to the distinguished public
position he held in his later years, is in-

deed a far cry, but from the letters to which we refer it is evident that amidst all the activities of his busy life and the great honours that came upon him at home and abroad he never lost his friendship or a certain spirit of deference for the grandson of Increase Mather, whom he had known more or less distantly in early life.

In the old letter-book of Doctor Byles's now owned by the New England Historic Genealogical Society, several letters from which we have been permitted to use, we find, undated, the following epistle, which must, however, have been written not long after Byles received his doctorate from the University of Aberdeen:

    "To the Honourable
   "D.ᴿ Benjamin Franklin
     "London.
"Sir;
 "It was with great Surprize and Pleasure, that I received your Picture from Philadelphia.

And it is with no little Pride, that when the
Picture introduces talk of the Original, a Theme
always pleasing to the Lovers of Learning, that
I can pronounce 'This was sent me by D.ͬ
Franklin himself.'

"But my Ambition has been strangely aug-
mented by a Copy of a Letter from London,
written by you to some unknown Person, in
which you Honour me with a Character so far
beyond any Merits of mine that I blush to read.
It was the utmost wish of one to be known only
by the Title of 'Sir Phillip Sidney's Friend.'
I can boast, and point to your own Hand to
prove it, that I have been at least *D.ͬ Franklin's* long Acquaintance. I had not the least
Apprehension that any Foreign Honours were
design'd me, till I was informed of it by a Letter
from your side of the Water; and received this
Transcript of your Friendship. My little offer-
ing of gratitude will make no perceptible
Addition to the Acknowledgements universally
paid you by the whole World of Literature and
Science.

"I should be exceedingly glad, Sir, if you
could be prevail'd on to furnish me with a
catalogue of your Publications. Those of them

that I am possess'd of are some of the most Agreeable Ornaments of my Library.

"Whatever Title my partial Friends may honour me with, none can more delight me than that of

"Dear Sir,
    "Your most Affectionate Friend
    "and obliged
        "humble Servant,
            [MATHER BYLES]

"The young Gentleman who brings you this, M͏ͬ *Edward Church*, is a Son of one of my Deacons. He has had a liberal Education in our college, but now visits *London* on affairs of merchandize. He will be pleased to see the Doctor he has read so much of.

"Shall I ask the Favour of you to forward the enclosed to *Aberdeen* with as little Expense as may be.

"I have just been reading a beautiful Letter of yours, written Feb. 22, 1756, on the Death of your Brother, which is handed about among us in Manuscript Copies. I am charmed with the Easy and Gay Light in which you view our Leaving this Little Earth, as Birds among the

Immortals : and as setting out on a party of
pleasure a little before our Friends are ready.
The Superstition with which we Seize and pre-
serve little accidental Touches of your pen,
puts one in mind of the care of the bishop to
collect the Jugs and Galipots with the paintings
of *Raphael.*"

On the 14th of May, 1787, Doctor Byles
wrote Franklin again :

"SIR,

"It is long since I had the pleasure of writing
to you by Mr Edward Church, to thank you
for your friendly mention of me in a letter that
I find was transmitted to the University of
Aberdeen. I doubt whether you ever received it,
under great weakness by old age and a palsy, I
seize this opportunity of employing my daughter
to repeat the thanks which I aimed to express in
that letter. Your Excellency is now the man
that I early expected to see you. I congratulate
my country upon her having produced a Franklin, and can only add, I wish to meet you where
complete felicity and we shall be for ever united.
I am my dear and early friend your most affectionate and humble servant,   "M. BYLES.

"P.S.   I refer you to the bearer, M.̃ Pier-
pont, to inform you how my life, and that of
my daughters, have been saved by your points."

The letter of Franklin's to the Principal
of King's College, Aberdeen, written from
Franklin's residence in Craven Street, London, for which Doctor Byles was so grate-
ful, was indeed a flattering letter.   It is
dated July 6, 1765, and is as follows:

"Sɪʀ,
"I have been acquainted many years with
the Rev. M.̃ Mather Byles, of whom you tell
me some account is desired.   He is a native of
New England, descended of the ancient Mather
Family, of which there have been two Doctors
in Divinity, both famous in that Country for
their learning and piety, Viz. Doctor Increase
Mather and Doctor Cotton Mather; the former
president of Harvard College at Cambridge.
This Mr. Byles was educated at that College,
where he distinguished himself by a close and
successful application to his studies; with the
usual degrees; and is now one of its Visitors or
Superintendents.   He is pastor of a Congre-

gational Church in Boston, the Capital of New
England. The principles or doctrines of those
Churches are the same with those of the
Church of Scotland, except what relates to
Church Government. He is a gentleman of
superior parts and learning; an eloquent
preacher and on many accounts an honour to
his Country.

"I am Sir your most humble Servant

"B. FRANKLIN."

In reply to Doctor Byles's letter of
May 14, 1787, Doctor Franklin wrote the
aged minister:

"PHIL^A June 1, 1788.

"DEAR OLD FRIEND,

"I duly received your kind Letter of May 14,
87. I was then busily engag'd in attending
our General Convention, which, added to the
ordinary current Business of this Government,
took up so much of my Time, that I was oblig'd
to postpone answering many Letters of Friends
which gave occasion of my mislaying some of
them, & among those was yours, only last
Week come again to hand. I think I never

o

receiv'd what you mention respecting the University of Aberdeen, but the Good will I might show on that Occasion was not of Importance enough to deserve your repeating the Acknowledgement. It was in me only paying a Debt; for I remember with Gratitude, that I owe one of my first Academical Honours to your Recommendation. It gives me much pleasure to understand that my Points have been of Service in the Protection of you and yours. I wish for your sake, that Electricity had really prov'd what it was at first suppos'd to be, a Cure for the palsy. It is however happy for you, that when Old Age and that Malady have concurr'd to infeeble you, and to disable you for Writing, you have a Daughter at hand to nurse you with *filial* attention, and to be your Secretary, of which I see she is very Capable, by the Elegance and Correctness of her Writing in the Letter I am answering. I too have a Daughter, who lives with me and is the Comfort of my declining Years, while my Son is estrang'd from me by the Part he took in the late War, and keeps aloof, residing in England, whose Cause he espous'd; whereby the old Proverb is exemplified:

"'My Son is my Son till he take him a
    Wife,
But my Daughter's my Daughter all Days of
    her Life.'

"I remember you had a little Collection of
Curiosities.   Please to honour with a Place in it
the inclosed Medal, which I got struck in Paris.
The Thought was much approv'd by the Con-
noiseurs there, and the Engraving well executed.
My best Wishes attend you, being ever your
affectionate Friend and humble Servant

"B. FRANKLIN." [64]

Eight years before this letter of Franklin's was written from Philadelphia, Doctor
Byles had given his grandson, Mather
Brown, on going to England, a letter to
Doctor Franklin, and as we shall see in a
later chapter, Franklin treated the young
painter with great cordiality, and introduced him "at Versailles as being grandson to one of his most particular friends in
America."

CHAPTER XI

LAST YEARS

OF Doctor Byles's life after the Revolution there is comparatively little to say. A lonely figure the old minister must have been as he went silently about the town, his friends among the crown officials and rich merchants far away, in England or in Nova Scotia, his son Mather also an exile in Halifax, his former parishioners passing him with averted eyes, and every prominent minister of his denomination, as indeed the town and state authorities and the new occupants of the confiscated houses of the proscribed Loyalists, regarding him as a traitor to the liberties of the people and returning with interest the scorn he had earlier visited on the champions of the popular cause. Under the most depressing

Dr. MATHER BYLES
From the original painting by Copley, 1767

circumstances, however, his wit never for-
sook him. In 1780 he gave his grandson,
Mather Brown, a letter to his old friend
Copley in England, which presumably in
reference to Copley's exalted position
abroad he addressed "To Mr. Copley in
the Solar System." For many years Doctor Samuel Cooper of the church in Brattle
Square had been a fellow-minister with
him in Boston and of course after the
Revolution that notably patriotic and
highly eloquent divine had little friendly
feeling toward the ex-minister of Hollis
Street. In his walks out of town Doctor
Cooper frequently passed Doctor Byles's
house, but never deigned to call. One
day Doctor Byles met Doctor Cooper
and said to him: "Doctor Cooper, you
treat me just like a baby!" "I hardly
take you, Sir," the Brattle Square minister with becoming dignity replied.
"Why," said the humorous Byles, "you
go by, by, by!" On the occurrence, May

19, 1780, of what was long known in
Boston as "the dark day," a lady in alarm
sent her young son to the doctor to know
if he could explain the terrifying phenom-
enon. "My dear," said Doctor Byles,
"tell your mother I am as much in the
dark as she is." "This for sententious
brevity," says the author of *Dealings with
the Dead*, "has never been surpassed, unless by the correspondence between the
comedian, Sam Foote, and his mother —
'Dear Sam, I'm in jail'; 'Dear Mother,
so am I.'"

Some time in 1783, Doctor Byles was
seized with paralysis, and from that time
until his death, some five years later, was
a confirmed and gradually failing invalid.
We have before spoken of the frequent
notices of him in the correspondence of
Doctor Jeremy Belknap, who was his
great-nephew, Belknap's mother having
been a daughter of one of Doctor Byles's
elder half-brothers.[65] In a letter to Ebe-

nezer Hazard of the 13ᵗʰ of December, 1783, Doctor Belknap says: "It is not usual with me to entertain you with an account of my bodily ails and complaints, but the situation I am now reduced to by an unlucky strain in my hip bears so near a resemblance to the state in which I lately found my *punning* uncle, Dr. Byles (who by the way, is the only surviving brother of Thomas Byles, late of Philadelphia, deceased) that I mention it for the sake of telling you one of *his* stories; and that I may give you a true idea of the man I will endeavour to relate it with its attendant circumstances. He is seventy-eight years old, and usually sits in an easy chair which has a back hung on hinges. In such a chair I found him sitting, and as I approached him he held out his hand. 'You must excuse my not getting up to receive you, cousin; for I am not one of the rising generation.'" Doctor Byles then went on to say, Doctor

Belknap says, that he had the same disease a good man he had once heard of had gone to his pastor, the Rev. M͏ʳ Willard, to complain of. M͏ʳ Willard was very fond of using scholastic terms and in a sermon shortly before had used the word synecdoche. Some one had told the man he had sciatica, and this word was so like synecdoche that the man felt sure the parson had used "sciatica" in his sermon and told him so. "I have," he said, "a disease the name of which you mentioned in your sermon on such a day. I cannot remember the word but it begins with *s*. M͏ʳ Willard looked over his notes and found synecdoche, and the man said, "Yes, that's it, I have synecdoche in my hip !"

In the great fire that raged in the south part of Boston in April, 1787, laying waste much of the region about Hollis Street, and burning the church, Doctor Byles's house was in so great danger that his

hoard of books, papers, prints, instruments, and most of his household goods,
were dislodged from their nearly fifty
years' repose and thrown out in chaotic
confusion in an adjoining green field.
Doctor Byles was taken for the night to
some hospitable house near by, but was
able to return to his own house the next
day.[66] One of the latest glimpses we get
of the old minister's mind is in the letter
he dictated to Doctor Franklin on the
14th of May, 1787, which we have given
at length on an earlier page.

It seems probable that after his dismissal from his church, Doctor Byles,
while he was able to walk, more or less
regularly worshipped with his daughters
at Trinity Church. It is doubtful if he
ever again entered a church of his own
denomination. While, as we have said,
he never so far as is recorded showed any
wish to enter the ministry of the Anglican
Church, as his son Mather, Jr., had long

before done, he could not have had any great dislike for the Prayer Book worship, and his friendship with Rev. Samuel Parker, Rector of Trinity, furnishes a presumption that he was more or less frequently seen at that Church. On the 5th of July, 1788, he died, and Doctor Sprague in his "Annals of the American Pulpit" says that Rev. Samuel Parker (afterwards Bishop Parker) was at his bedside shortly before the end came. Probably in allusion to friendly controversies the two had had on the subject of a threefold ministry, Doctor Byles in an almost inaudible voice said to his friend as he bent over him: "I have almost got to that world where there are no bishops !" "I hoped, Doctor," said Mr. Parker kindly, "that you were going to the Shepherd and Bishop of Souls." The *Massachusetts Centinel* of Wednesday, July 9, 1788, says briefly: "Died on Saturday last, the Reverend Doctor Byles, aged 81."

The body of the aged divine was laid to rest in tomb No. 2 in the Granary Burying Ground, but whether Rev. Samuel Parker performed the burial service or not we cannot tell.[67]

July 17, 1788, Ebenezer Hazard writes Doctor Belknap facetiously: "So the old Doctor has left off punning at last. What must the grave spirits in heaven think on the approach of so ludicrous an one as his."[68] September 14, 1790, Doctor Belknap writes Hazard: "I add for your amusement and for a laugh among a few friends, a number of articles found in the house of the late Dr Byles." These he enumerates as, five or six dozen pairs of spectacles, "of all powers and all fashions"; more than twenty walking sticks, "of different sizes and contrivances," about a dozen jest-books, several packs of cards, "new and clean," a quantity of whetstones, bones, etc., "as much as a man could carry in a bushel basket on his shoulder,"

a large number of weights for shops,
money-scales, etc., "some in sets, and
some broken," a large collection of pictures from Hogarth's celebrated prints,
"down to the corners of newspapers and
pieces of linen." He says also there was
a large parcel of coins, "from Tiberius
Caesar to Massachusetts cents," a parcel
of children's toys, — among these two bags
of marbles, a quantity of Tom Thumb
books and puerile histories, — about a dozen
bird-cages and rat-traps, a set of gardeners'
tools and one of carpenters' tools, a parcel
of speaking-trumpets and hearing tubes,
with many other things. The miscellaneous
character of Doctor Byles's accumulations
during his lifetime, which caused Doctor Belknap so much amusement, is fully borne
out by the recorded inventory of Byles's
estate.

CHAPTER XII

THE BYLES FAMILY

BY his first wife, as we have said, Doctor Byles had six children, three of whom, Mather, Jr., Elizabeth, and Samuel, lived to grow up; by his second wife he had three, two of whom only, the Misses Mary and Catherine lived to maturity. Mather Byles, Jr., was born in Boston January twelfth, 1734,[69] and graduated at Harvard College in 1751. Six years later he formally entered the Congregational ministry at New London, Connecticut, over the church in which town he remained for between ten and eleven years. At his ordination his father preached the sermon and gave the charge, and a very impressive and serious sermon and charge these efforts of the older Mather Byles were. The sermon as printed is entitled "The man of God thoroughly furnished to every good work," and it is a strong and earnest presentation of the minister's duty and opportunity. To his first ministerial charge the youthful Byles brought the prestige of his distinguished Mather descent, his father's ecclesiastical, social, and literary importance, and his own education and brilliant promise, and naturally he at once became a great favourite in the Connecticut town. The chief cause of discomfort to him in| New London for a long time was the presence there of an obscure Sabbatarian sect known as the Rogerenes, with which people he soon began a violent controversy, chiefly on the question of the special day that should be observed as the day of rest. We have a portrait of the younger Byles taken, it would seem, soon after the Revolution, when he was about forty-five years old, which shows him, as he was, a man of

Dr. MATHER BYLES, Jr.

From the original painting

somewhat delicate mould, probably smaller
than his father, with a nervous, excitable
face, rather thin lips, firmly pressed together, and the unmistakable look and
pose of an aristocratic feeling man. On
the 12th of May, 1761, Byles married at
Roxbury, Massachusetts, his second cousin,
Rebecca Walter, a daughter of the Rev.
Nathaniel Walter of that place, whose
older sister Sarah was married to Sir
Robert Hazelrigg, a Leicestershire bar-
onet, and whose brother William when a
few years out of Harvard embraced Epis-
copacy, went to London for ordination,
and a little later became Rector of Boston's
Trinity Church.

It is not to any one difficult in these days
to see why the younger Mather Byles should
not have remained always a Congregation-
alist. He had in Boston probably associated almost as much with Episcopalians
as with Congregationalists, and he was the
sort of man to whom a classical liturgy and

dignified ecclesiastical ceremonial would naturally strongly appeal. For the last three years of his New London pastorate he was, he says, at heart virtually an Episcopalian, and at length in April, 1768, he formally so declared himself to the people of his charge. In some way his change of feeling had become known in Boston, and suddenly, quite unexpectedly to him, he announced, the wardens and vestry of Christ Church had given him an invitation to become their Rector instead of minister of the New London Congregational Church. His statement of this fact and of his wish immediately to sever his connection with the Congregationalists was received by his church with profound amazement and disgust. The people at first strongly remonstrated with him, but when they found that his mind was made up, they bitterly denounced and mercilessly ridiculed him, and on their church book recorded angrily that "the Rev. Mather Byles had *dismist himself* from the congregation." To the moment of his resignation of his pastorate his popularity had been general, but now in the streets could be heard a wretched doggerel song on his conversion, called "The Proselyte," sung to the tune of the "Thief and Cordelier," while into general circulation from some local press came a "Wonderful Dream," in which the spirit of the venerable Richard Mather was introduced rebuking his great-grandson for his degenerate apostasy from the Puritan faith. On his part M: Byles regarded the call from Christ Church as "manifestly a call of Providence inviting him to a greater sphere of usefulness, and plainly pointing out to him the path of duty," and at once he left New London for Boston, thence sailing for England, to be reordained a priest of the Anglican Church.

In Episcopal Orders he soon came back to his native town and began his pastorate

P

in Boston as Rector of Christ Church, and in this rectorship he remained until the 18th of April, 1775. On that day he formally resigned this charge, his resignation probably being due largely to the fact that his royalist sympathies had become too pronounced to allow him to remain with a people, the majority of whom desired separation from the British empire. The excuse he gave for resigning, however, was that he had received a call from St. John's Church, Portsmouth, New Hampshire, to become Rector there. To the Portsmouth church for some reason he did not go, but when Howe's fleet sailed from Boston in March, 1776, he with his children, in company with his brother-in-law, William Walter, Rector of Trinity, and the Rev. Doctor Caner, Rector of King's Chapel, went with the great body of Boston Tories to Halifax, and there was soon appointed, assistant to Rev. Doctor Breynton, Rector of St. Paul's

Church, and chaplain to the British troops.
In May, 1789, he removed to St. John,
New Brunswick, in that town assuming
the rectorship of Trinity Church, and as
in Halifax, the garrison chaplaincy as
well.

Rev. Mather Byles, Jr., took his master's degree at Harvard, in course, in 1754,
and from Yale College received a similar
degree in 1757. In 1770 the University
of Oxford conferred on him a doctorate in
divinity. He married three times, first
as we have said his second cousin, Rebecca
Walter, second, in Halifax, another second
cousin, Sarah, daughter of Byfield Lyde,
third, also in Halifax, the widow of an
officer, M^rs. Susanna Reid. By his first
wife Rebecca, who died a little over four
months before he left Boston for Halifax,
he had nine children, by his second wife
four, and from him, in later generations,
not a few important people in the British
Colonies have been descended. For the

most part, however, these have borne other names than Byles.[70]

Of the tender relations that always existed between Mather Byles, Jr., and his father we gain sufficient idea from one of the last letters that the aged Hollis Street minister ever wrote. On the 22^d of February, 1787, Mrs Sarah Lyde Byles died in Halifax, and the 14th of the following April the senior Doctor Byles by the hand of one of his daughters wrote his widowed son:

"MY DEARLY BELOVED SON AND FIRST BORN,

"I am unable to write a Word, but my tender sympathy with you compels me to attempt to dictate. I feel for your Distresses, but can only carry you afresh to Him into whose hand I have so many thousand times committed you. You Preach to others, Preach now to yourself. Carry my tenderest Blessings to Mather and my other Dear Grandchildren, whom I leave in the kind Hands of my Lord Jesus, I am

"Your most affectionate and dying Parent
"M. BYLES."

Doctor Byles's daughter Elizabeth, born
March twenty-second, 1737, was married
as his second wife, in 1760, to Gawen
Brown of Boston, a noted maker of watches
and clocks,[71] and became the mother of
Mather Brown, a painter of some note,
born October seventh, 1761, who in 1780
left Boston for London, with letters from
his grandfather to Copley and Doctor
Benjamin Franklin. Brown's later success in London was probably due in great
measure to the fact that through Franklin
he came almost immediately to the favourable notice of Benjamin West. When he
reached London, West was in Paris, and
thither Brown almost immediately went.
In a letter home in 1781 he writes: "D.[r]
Franklin has given me a pass, and recom-
mendatory letter to the famous M.[r] West.
He treats me with the utmost politeness;
has given me an invitation to his home.
I delivered him my grandfather's message,
he expressed himself with the greatest

esteem and affection for him, and has since introduced me at Versailles, as being grandson to one of his most particular friends in America." In another letter Brown writes: "In consequence of the recommendation of D.̇ Franklin, who gave me letters to his fellow-townsman, the famous D.̇ West of Philadelphia, I practise gratis with this gentleman, who affords me every encouragement, as well as M.̇ Copley, who is particularly kind to me, welcomed me to his home, and lent me his pictures, etc. At my arrival M.̇ Treasurer Gray carried me and introduced me to Lord George Germaine."

As a pupil of West, Brown studied some time in Paris, but in 1782, and thereafter for fifty years, he painted and exhibited at the Royal Academy in London. In England he painted, besides many noted military and naval officers and other commoners, King George Third and Queen Charlotte, and the *Gentleman's Magazine*

MATHER BROWN
From the original painting by himself

styles him "Historical Painter to His
Majesty and the late Duke of York." In
his last years Brown grew eccentric and
lived in a forlorn way; his death occurred
in London on the 25th of May, 1831.

Doctor Byles's sixth and last child by
his first wife was Samuel, born twenty-
third of March, 1743, who studied medi-
cine and seems to have already reached
his profession when he died, June six-
teenth, 1764. After his death his father
published a little volume called "Pious
Remains of a Young Gentleman lately
Deceased," the book consisting of a touch-
ing prose epistle to one of his half-sisters
whom he calls "Aminta," in which he
gives a fervid imaginary account of the
experiences of his own sister, Elizabeth,
immediately after she died ; and eight
selected poems, the whole prefaced no
doubt by Doctor Byles, his father, and
the preface bearing date July seventh,
1764.

When Doctor Byles died his only living descendants in Boston were his two younger daughters, the Misses Mary and Catherine Byles. Of these ladies in their earliest youth we hear very little, but at the time of the Revolution they come before us in a rather clear and entirely picturesque way. In 1775 Miss Mary was twenty-five and Miss Catherine twenty-two, and while the siege was in progress the British officers of highest rank, as we have shown, seem to have been frequent visitors at their father's house; one of these visitors being Earl Percy, whose letters from Boston to his father, the Duke of Northumberland, and to the Rev. Doctor Percy, editor of the noted "Reliques of Ancient Poetry," a distant relative of the Earl, were recently published in Boston. To the end of their days the Miss Byleses were staunch royalists, and among their most cherished recollections were the flattering attentions they

Miss CATHERINE BYLES
From the original painting by Henry Pelham

had received from Lord Howe and Earl
Percy during the siege. Of Earl Percy
they remembered with satisfaction that
he had not only once ordered them sere-
naded by a regimental band, but on some
still happier occasion had promenaded with
them arm-in-arm on the fashionable Mall.
The Miss Byleses lived, Mary until
October 1, 1832, Catherine until July 19,
1837, the former dying at over eighty-two,
the latter at almost eighty-four, and for
many years before their deaths they were
regarded, as indeed they were, as lonely
relics of a period very remote in Boston's
social history.

Some time before the death of Miss
Mary Byles, Miss Eliza Leslie, of whom
we have already spoken, sister of Charles
Robert Leslie the painter, came to Boston
to visit, and in January and February,
1842, in *Graham's Magazine*, as we have
said, she published some interesting
reminiscences of a visit she was permitted

to make to these ancient spinsters. Miss Mary she describes as "a rather broad-framed and very smiling old lady, habited in a black worsted petticoat and a short gown, into the neck of which was tucked a book-muslin kerchief. Her silver hair was smoothly arranged over a wrinkled but well-formed forehead, beneath which twinkled two small blue eyes. Her head was covered with a close, full-bordered white linen cap, that looked equally convenient for night or for day." "Miss Catherine was unlike her elder sister, both in figure and face, her features being much sharper (in fact excessively sharp), and her whole person extremely thin. She also was arrayed in a black bombasin petticoat, a short gown, and a close lined cap, with a deep border, that seemed almost to bury her narrow visage." The old ladies kept no regular servant, and when visitors arrived Miss Mary always came to the door. Miss Catherine, however,

BOSTON COMMON

From an engraving by Samuel Hill, 1789

unfailingly produced her own effect by not making her appearance till callers had sat for some time in the parlour. Naturally the conversation of both sisters was much of the past, and always, as Miss Leslie says, "they gloried, they triumphed, in the firm adherence of their father and his family to the royalty of England, and scorned the idea of even now being classed among the *citoyennes* of a republic, a republic, which, as they said, they had never acknowledged and never would; regarding themselves still as faithful subjects to His Majesty of Britain, whoever that majesty might be." To Miss Leslie these ancient ladies expressed much regret that they had not been able to prevail on their father after the Revolution to renounce America entirely and remove with his family to England, in which case, said Miss Mary, they should all have been introduced at court and the King and Queen would have spoken to them and thanked them kindly for their loyalty. In Boston it was a matter of common knowledge that on the accession of William the Fourth one of the sisters had humbly addressed his sailor Majesty, assuring him that the family of Doctor Byles of Boston had never renounced their loyalty to the throne of England and never would.

One of the most conspicuous treasures of these ancient ladies was a handsome chair, brought from England long before by their grandfather, Lieutenant-Governor Tailer, on the top of which was carved a royal crown. As a special favour each visitor was permitted to sit a moment in this chair, and always the hostesses' exclamation, as the privileged person took his seat, was: "We wonder that you, a republican, can sit comfortably under the crown!" Of their revered father, and other members of their family, living or dead, the Miss Byleses had many reminiscences, some of their father's witty sayings they being especially proud to repeat. For their absent nephew, Mather Brown, they had deep affection, and of course no one was ever suffered to forget that this moderately successful portrait painter had the very great honour of having painted members of the Royal Family. On the walls of their parlour hung the notable portraits of Doctor Byles which we have described, the latest of the two Copleys having the greatest value in their eyes, not because of its general intrinsic merit but because it portrayed faithfully their father's cornelian ring. "My eyes," says Miss Leslie, "were soon riveted on a fine portrait of Doctor Mather Byles, from the wonderful pencil of Copley. . . . The moment I looked at this picture I knew it must be a likeness, for I saw in its lineaments the whole character of Doctor Byles, particularly the covert humour of the eye. The face was pale, the features well-formed, and the aspect pleasantly acute. He was represented in his ecclesiastical habiliments, with a curled and powdered wig. On his finger was a signet ring containing a very fine red cornelian. While I was contemplating the admirably depicted countenance his daughters were both very voluble in directing attention to the cornelian ring, which they evidently considered the best part of the picture; declaring it to be an exact likeness of that very ring, and just as natural as life." In the Byles parlour also hung an attractive portrait of Mather Brown by himself, and in other parts of the house portraits of the Miss Byleses themselves, in the freshness of young maidenhood.

From the time of their father's dismissal from the pastorate of the Hollis Street Church, and perhaps before, the Byles sisters had worshipped at Trinity Church, their Rector at first being the Rev. Samuel Parker, who in 1804 became the second Episcopal bishop of Massachu-

setts,[72] and as long as their health permitted
they went to service regularly on Sundays,
dressed with slight regard for changing
fashions, and closely veiled, "not so much
for concealment as for gentility." During
many of their declining years, however,
they rarely went, otherwise, far beyond
their own door. In their wills they remembered scrupulously by name each of
a considerable number of their brother's
descendants in England or in Canada, and
on the death of Miss Catherine, as had
been agreed between the sisters before
Miss Mary died, the treasures of the old
house on Tremont Street, of which there
were not a few, were almost without exception removed directly to Halifax, Nova
Scotia, where some of the most valuable
of them still remain.

NOTES

[1] Sprague's "Annals of the American Pulpit" and other works which mention D: Byles say that he was tall, well-proportioned, and altogether of commanding presence, that his voice was at once melodious and powerful, and that his manner of address both in public and in private was highly pleasing.

CHAPTER II

[2] Reverend D: Samuel Mather, in consequence of serious disaffection against him in the Old North Church, in 1742 led off a portion of the church and formed a new church, with a meeting house at the corner of Hanover and North Bennet streets. This church, however, lasted only until shortly after Samuel Mather's death in 1785.

[3] Reverend D: Increase Mather was ordained over the Old North Church, May 27, 1664, and died still as its chief pastor, August 23, 1723.

[4] D: Cotton Mather's Diary, Vol. 2, p. 64.

[5] Before the close of the 17th century no less than ten members of the Mather family had been graduated at Harvard.

[6] His master's degree came in course three years later.

[7] One of these was Josiah Smith of Charleston, South Carolina, the first student from the Carolinas to come to Harvard, the other was Thomas Clap of Scituate.

⁸ Dʳ Byles's uncle Cotton Mather was not ordained until seven years after graduation.

⁹ See Joseph T. Buckingham's "Specimens of Newspaper Literature: with Personal Memoirs, Anecdotes, and Reminiscences," Boston, 1850.

¹⁰ In an address to the public in the *Boston Gazette* of January 29, 1722, Increase Mather attacks the *Courant*, calling its statement that he had been a supporter of that paper a wicked libel and saying: "I cannot but pity poor Franklin, who tho' but a *Young Man* it may be Speedily he must appear before the Judgment Seat of God, and what answer will he give for printing things so vile and abominable? And I cannot but Advise the Supporters of this Courant to consider the Consequences of being *Partakers in other Men's Sins*, and no more Countenance such a Wicked *Paper*."

¹¹ *The New England Weekly Journal* in its initial number announced that it intended publishing the most remarkable occurrences, both foreign and domestic, of the time. It bore the imprint, first of S. Kneeland, then of S. Kneeland and T. Green.

¹² Dʳ Cotton Mather died February 13, 1728; his father, Dʳ Increase Mather, died, as we have before noted, between four and five years earlier.

CHAPTER III

¹³ Honorable Jonathan Belcher was Governor of Massachusetts for eleven years. In the "Belcher Papers" (Mass. Hist. Coll., 6ᵗʰ Series, Vols. 6 and 7) we find some interesting correspondence between Governor Belcher in Boston and Mʳ Thomas Hollis in London concerning the

organization of the parish and the building and furnishing
of the Hollis Street Church. October 5, 1733, the Governor, who calls himself "chief patron" of the church,
writes : "Upon laying out a considerable tract of land in
this town about two years ago into streets and house lots,
one of the main streets was named Hollis Street, since
which a number of worthy men have erected and finish'd
a handsome c^{hh}, whereof the Revd Mr Mather Byles
was ordain'd the pastor in Decemb^r last. He is grandson to the late Rev^d learned and excellent Dr Increase
Mather. Altho' this new congregation are a number of
sober good Christians, yet they are not in the most plenti-
full circumstances, and I have promist to mention to you
the procuring for them by yourself & friends a small bell
for this new c^{hh} in Hollis Street." The bell was given
by Mr. Hollis in 1734, and was "generally thought the
best in this country." The same year a handsome clock
was placed in the interior. May 2, 1742, Dr Byles
formally presented to the church, from Hon. William Dummer, late lieutenant-governor, "a large and rich folio
Bible, on condition that it should be read as a part of
publick worship on the Lord's day among us." The congregation voted their thanks to Mr Dummer for this
"stately church Bible," and May 9, 1742, reading from
the Scriptures was introduced in the church.

[14] "History of the Old South Church," by Hamilton
Andrews Hill (1890), Vol. I, p. 461.

[15] Dr Byles scrupulously mentions the place of his
wedding in the family record which he kept. It is doubtful whether the Congregationalists at this time often
celebrated marriages in their meeting-houses.

¹⁶ Pelham and Smibert were then painting in Boston, Copley having not yet come on this earthly scene.

¹⁷ Proceedings of the Massachusetts Historical Society, 1860–1862, pp. 124–126.

¹⁸ This witticism of Dᴿ Byles also comes to us as follows: "Your taste in distempers must be very bad when it has led you to prefer Quincy to Byles."

¹⁹ There seems little doubt that this early love affair of Dᴿ Byles's was with Elizabeth Wendell, daughter of Abraham and Katarina (De Key) Wendell, who was baptized August 20, 1704, and was married April 15, 1725, to Edmund Quincy. Writing from Boston to his friend Ebenezer Hazard on the 24ᵗʰ of March, 1788, Dᴿ Byles's grand-nephew, Jeremy Belknap, says of Judge Quincy's end: "Old Daddy Quincy died here about the time that you mention Dᴿ Crosby did at New York. He was buried the day before Dᴿ Byles." — "Belknap Papers," Part 2, Mass. Hist. Soc. Coll., Vol. 3, 5ᵗʰ Series, p. 52.

CHAPTER IV

²⁰ At the same time Dᴿ Byles's wife Anna was received from the Brattle Street Church.

²¹ Mʳˢ Belcher was a daughter of Lieutenant-Governor William Partridge of New Hampshire.

²² We have seen this ponderous sermon, delivered October 17, 1736, in which Dᴿ Prince discusses not only the natural history of death, but the views of death and the future held by Greek and Roman philosophers, and many other classes of men, including the slaves of Africa and the North American Indians, and in which he gives a minute account of many deaths by earthquakes, plagues,

deluges, and conflagrations, since the time of Christ. As we read the sermon we cannot help being amazed that in any age people could have sat patiently through such a fearful discourse.

[23] "Yankee heraldry," writes Professor Barrett Wendell, "has never been punctilious. Long before the Revolution people who found themselves prosperous were apt to adopt armorial bearings, often far from grammatical, which are still reverently preserved on silver, tombstones, and embroidered hatchments." — "A Literary History of America," p. 243.

[24] These three were Mather, Jr., Elizabeth, who became the wife of Gawen Brown, and Samuel, a young physician, who died June 16, 1764, aged slightly over twenty-one, having written a little prose and poetry, which his father printed after his death.

[25] The burial place of the Byles family from this time was Tomb No. 2 in the Granary Burying Ground, built by Dr Oliver Noyes, Anna Byles's father, in 1720, at the same time that Governor Belcher built his tomb in this cemetery.

[26] Hon. William Tailer's death had occurred at Dorchester, March 8, 1732 (new style).

[27] Dr. Byles paid for the property £350, the estate being described as "all that certain messuage, tenement or dwelling-house, with the land thereto belonging, situate, lying, and being at the southerly end of Boston aforesaid, butted and bounded as follows . . . together with all and singular the houses, out-houses, edifices, buildings, easements, and fences thereon standing." This was the first property the Suffolk Deeds record Mather Byles as

having owned. The bend in the road where the house stood was long known as "Byles's Corner."

At some time late in the lives of the Miss Byleses the Byles property was described by Mr. Nathaniel Bradlee as "One old dwelling-house in the town of Boston, two stories high, built of wood, $18\frac{1}{2}$ feet front and 38 feet deep. The lot of land measures 135 feet front and 81 feet deep, containing in the whole about 11,800 square feet, a great part of which is unimproved. The house itself is so much decayed from age as to be scarcely tenantable. This estate belongs to Misses M. and C. Byles, and has never been taxed by the town." In 1838, after the death of Miss Catherine Byles, the property in Tremont Street was sold at auction to a Roxbury man bearing the familiar name of Harrison Gray.

[28] " Cards of Boston
containing a
Variety of facts and descriptions
relative to that City
In past and present times;
so arranged as to form
An Instructive and Amusing Game
for young people
By Miss Leslie.

(Entered according to Act of Congress in the Clerk's office in the District of Massachusetts, 1831, by Munroe and Francis.) "

[29] The baptisms of all Dr Byles's children were performed by their father, who recorded them lovingly on his church register as of "my Mather," or "my Belcher," or

"my Samuel," "first, second, or third child," as the case might be.

[30] The late Rev. D! Henry S. Nash once said trenchantly to his class in Cambridge that a certain pious church father "had lived too much with godly women."

CHAPTER V

[31] The persons who, November 14, 1732, subscribed the Covenant as the original members were : John Clough, Joseph Payson, Henry Gibbon, James Day, Jonathan Neal, Hopestill Foster, Ebenezer Clough, Nathaniel Fairfield, John Cravath, and Alden Bass, all of whom had been in communion with other churches. Besides these there were John Blake, Thomas Trott, and Isaac Loring, who then for the first time were received into full communion.

[32] See "Some Aspects of the Religious Life of New England, with Special Reference to Congregationalists," by George Leon Walker, D.D., 1897.

[33] "I can't suppose," says Rev. Samuel Phillips of Andover, "that any one . . . who at all times faithfully improves the common grace he has, that is to say, is diligent in attending on the appointed means of grace, with a desire to profit thereby . . . shall perish for want of special and saving grace."

[34] In 1741 the number of persons admitted was six, in 1742 thirteen, in 1743 five, and in 1744 nine.

[35] The Rev. Samuel A. Eliot, D.D., says in a preface to "Pioneers of Religious Liberty in America" (1903) : "Two hundred and seventy-two years ago John Cotton, minister of the First Church in Boston, with the coöperation of his

ministerial associates established what came to be known as the 'Great and Thursday Lecture.' This weekly lecture was in colonial times the chief social and religious event in Boston."

[36] Three other ministers of Boston, Dr Chauncy, Dr Samuel Cooper, and Dr Andrew Eliot, had received their doctorates from the University of Edinburgh. The Rev. Ebenezer Pemberton, Jr., had received his from Princeton. Before 1771 Harvard had given the degree of S.T.D. only once; this was in 1692, to Increase Mather. In 1771 Harvard gave it next to Rev. Nathaniel Appleton of Cambridge, who had graduated in 1712.

[37] See an article by James R. Gilmore ("Edmund Kirke") in the *New England Magazine* for August, 1897, on "Nathaniel Emmons and Mather Byles." Dr Emmons was pastor of the Second Church, Wrentham. In this article the writer gives a pleasant account of the relations between Dr Emmons and Dr Byles, as Dr Emmons himself had described them to him. In the same issue of the *New England Magazine* is a poem of twelve stanzas by Henry Ames Blood, entitled "The Byles Girls" (the two daughters of Dr Byles).

Chapter VI

[38] Dr Isaac Watts lived between 1674 and 1748, Alexander Pope between 1688 and 1744. Johnson says of Lansdowne: "He had no ambition above the imitation of Waller, of whom he has copied the faults and very little more."

[39] So far as we can learn, Pope never wrote Dr Byles more than one letter. We have not seen this letter, but it

is said that although Dr Byles used to show it with pride, it had not a remarkably pleasant tone. Dr Byles had apparently sent Pope some of his own verses, for Pope remarks with some irony that he had feared the Muses had forsaken England, but it was evident they had only taken up their abode in the new world. Dr Byles's latest letter to Pope, preserved in his letter book, is entirely wanting in the effervescent praise of his earlier letters.

Chapter VII

[40] "Memorial History of Boston," Vol. 2, pp. 425–427.

[41] Mr. Sargent calls Dr Byles's humour "that frolicsome vein which was to him as congenital as is the tendency of a fish to swim."

[42] See for this ballad the New England Historic Genealogical Register, Vol. 13, p. 131.

[43] Mackintosh is said to have rolled on the floor in an agony of laughter at one of Sydney Smith's jokes.

[44] See "Drake's Landmarks of Boston." This story is also given as follows: The architecture of King's Chapel was unfamiliar to Bostonians generally and was at first much ridiculed. When Dr Byles *saw the building erected*, with some sarcasm he made the remark we have given here.

[45] "Memorial History of Boston," Vol. 2, p. 482, and elsewhere.

[46] Dr Belknap tells it in its briefer form in a letter to Ebenezer Hazard, dated August 28, 1780.

[47] Joseph Green, a Boston merchant of considerable fortune, is said to have had also the largest private library in New England. At the Revolution he was appointed

a mandamus councillor, though he never took the oath. Later he was proscribed and banished, and we find him among the twenty-two members of the Loyalist Club who met weekly in London, where he spent his last years. A crayon portrait of him was made by Copley. In the earlier part of his life, when he was unfriendly towards Governor Belcher, he was not so conservative in his political views as he afterward became.

[48] This allusion is of course to Dr. Byles's cat, on whose death Green had written an elegy.

[49] For this passage at arms between Byles and Green, see Duyckinck's "Cyclopædia of American Literature," and Mass. Hist. Soc. Coll., 5th. Series, Vol. 2, pp. 70–73.

CHAPTER VIII

[50] The friend was James R. Gilmore ("Edmund Kirke"). See in the *New England Magazine* for August, 1897, the article we have before mentioned on "Nathaniel Emmons and Mather Byles."

[51] For the dramatic ending of Dr. Byles's pastorate, see a sketch of Joseph May in the N. E. Hist. and Gen. Register, Vol. 27, p. 116; and the "Belknap, Papers" in the Mass. Hist. Soc. Coll., Vol. 4, p. 107.

[52] See Mass. Hist. Collections, 6th. Series, Vol. 4, pp. 122, 123, and pp. 106, 107.

[53] "Historical Notices," by Ephraim Eliot, quoted in the "History of the Old South Church," Vol. 2, p. 186.

CHAPTER IX

[54] Mass. Hist. Coll., 6 Series, Vol. 4, part 3, p. 122, note.

[55] Dr. Ezra Stiles's "Literary Diary," Vol. 2, p. 168.

[56] Dᴿ Mather Byles, Jr., had written Mr. Bailey from Halifax, under date of February 17, 1778, telling him that he (Bailey) was entitled to apply for fifty pounds to an English fund for the relief of distressed clergymen in America. — "Life of Rev. Jacob Bailey, the Frontier Missionary."

[57] Rev. John Eliot was a sprightly letter writer and his letters are none the less entertaining because of the writer's positive opinions. It would seem as if both he and Jeremy Belknap may have had some personal grudge against Dᴿ Byles.

[58] "Memorial History of Boston," Vol. 3, p. 160.

[59] See Knox's portrait in the third volume of the "Memorial History of Boston."

[60] See "Dealings with the Dead," and Drake's "History of Boston," pp. 746–748. The former reports Dᴿ Byles as saying when he saw the troops: "Well, I think we can no longer complain that our grievances are not red-dressed!"

CHAPTER X

[61] It will be remembered that some of the leading Tory families, like the Brinleys and Royalls, who were obliged to leave Massachusetts at the time of the Revolution, lived chiefly out of town, in Cambridge, Roxbury, or Medford.

[62] Franklin was born January 17, 1706, and died April 17, 1790.

[63] The *New-England Courant* was first issued August 7, 1721, the only earlier Boston newspapers having been the *Boston News-Letter*, begun in 1704, and the *Boston Gazette*, started in 1719. With these two papers the

Courant ran along until June 4, 1726, when it stopped. Between February 11, 1723, and July 20, 1724, it was nominally printed by Benjamin Franklin in Queen Street; from July 27, 1724, until June 4, 1726, it was issued in Union Street, still in Benjamin Franklin's name. Benjamin, however, finally left Boston, in October, 1723.

[64] This letter is printed in "D? Franklin's Life and Letters." It appeared also in "The Bower of Taste," March 1, 1828.

CHAPTER XI

[65] D? Jeremy Belknap, the eminent historian and liberal theologian, was the eldest child of Joseph and Sarah (Byles) Belknap. He was born in Boston June 4, 1744, and died June 20, 1798. In 1765, when he was debating whether he should enter the ministry or not, in distress of mind he wrote his great-uncle expressing his fear that he was not fit spiritually for the ministerial office. To the young man's frank letter D? Byles replied in the kindliest and most judicious and Christian way that while he is glad of the deep piety his nephew shows he feels that he is mistakenly writing bitter things against himself. "My dear Child," he tenderly says, "it is with a mixture of pleasure and sorrow that I read your letter. I am pleased to see your great care not to enter the ministry in a state of unrenewed nature; and I am grieved at your censure upon yourself." "May God bless you, my Son," the writer closes, "and sanctify and comfort you; and introduce you with the noblest preparation into the ministry. So prays your affectionate M. Byles." To this kindly letter Belknap replies asking

his uncle to pray that he might not be mistaken in a matter of such everlasting importance; that he might not build on a false foundation.

[66] See the "Belknap Papers," Vol. 1, p. 470; "Memorial History of Boston," Vol, 3, p. 7; "History of the Old South Church," Vol. 2, p. 240.

[67] A declaration made by the daughters of D: Byles in connexion with the settlement of their father's estate includes the statement that a number of their friends "raised a sum of money by subscription to defray the expenses of his funeral without any charge to the estate."

[68] Mass. Hist. Coll., 3, 51.

CHAPTER XII

[69] His father baptized him, recording the baptism affectionately as of "my Mather." He graduated at Harvard, as we have said, in 1751, but his ordination at New London did not take place until November 18, 1757. What he was doing from 1751 to 1755 we do not know, but from 1755 to 1757 he was (the 37th) librarian of Harvard College. See "Library of Harvard University, Biographical Contributions," Edited by Justin Winsor, No. 52; "The Librarians of Harvard College 1667–1877," by Alfred Claghorn Potter and Charles Knowles Bolton, Cambridge, 1897. In the *Boston Evening-Post* of May 2, 1768, we read: "On Friday last the Rev. Mr. Mather Byles, and Family, came to Town from New London; and we hear he embarks in the first Vessel for England, in order to receive Episcopal Ordination to qualify himself for Minister of Christ Church here, from whom he received an invitation, as lately mentioned."

At the evacuation of Boston, with seventeen other Anglican clergymen he went to Halifax, one of these clergymen being the Rev. D.ʳ Caner, "bent with bodily infirmities and in his seventy-seventh year." A letter from D.ʳ Caner soon after, from Halifax, says: "As to the Clergy of Boston, indeed, they have for eleven months past been exposed to difficulty and distress in every shape; and as to myself, having determined to maintain my post as long as possible, I continued to officiate to the small remains of my parishioners, though without a support, till the 10ᵗʰ of March, when I suddenly and unexpectedly received notice that the King's troops would immediately evacuate the town. It is not easy to paint the distress and confusion of the inhabitants on this occasion. I had but six or seven hours allowed to prepare for the measure, being obliged to embark the same day for Halifax, where we arrived the 1ˢᵗ of April. This sudden movement prevented me from saving my books, furniture or any part of my interest, except bedding, wearing apparel, and a little provision for my small family during the passage.

"I am now at Halifax with my daughter and servant, but without any means of support, except what I receive from the benevolence of the worthy D.ʳ Breynton."

⁷⁰ The well-known Nova Scotia families of Almon, Des Brisay, and Ritchie, are among his descendants.

⁷¹ Elizabeth Byles was married to Gawen Brown a little more than three months after Brown's first wife died. The Hollis Street Church records state that Gawen Brown was admitted to that church on a letter of recommendation from a Dissenting Church at Framlington, in

Northumberland, August 10, 1760. He married first,
April 5, 1750 (Rev. Joseph Sewall) Mary Flagg, who died
March 28, 1760, and was buried in the Granary Burying
Ground, after having borne her husband six children, all
of whom were baptized in the Old South. Brown married,
second, July 3, 1760 (intention June 18, 1760), Elizabeth
Byles, who bore her husband one son, Mather, baptized
October 11, 1761. Elizabeth died June 6, 1763, her death
evidently plunging the Byles family in deep grief. Octo-
ber 19, 1764, Gawen Brown married third, in the New
South parish, Elizabeth (Hill) Adams, widow of Dᵣ Joseph
Adams, brother of Samuel Adams the patriot. Brown
died August 8, 1801, aged 82. See notes on Gawen and
Mather Brown by Frederick L. Gay in Mass. Hist. Soc.
Proceedings, XLVII, pp. 289, 293 (March–April, 1914).

[72] It was owing to the Christian thoughtfulness of Rev.
Dᵣ Andrew Eliot of the New North Church, who, we have
stated, was one of the three Congregational ministers who
stayed in Boston during the siege, that Rev. Samuel
Parker did not go away with the other Anglican clergymen when Howe evacuated the town. The Rector of
Trinity Church at the time was the Rev. Dᵣ William
Walter, a brother-in-law of Rev. Mather Byles, Jr., and
his assistant was the Rev. Samuel Parker. When the
word was given that the Tories must leave, Dᵣ Caner, Dᵣ
Walter, and Rev. Mather Byles, Jr., at once took refuge
with Howe's fleet, and Mr. Parker also was packing his
books to go. Dᵣ Eliot had been an opponent of Epis-
copacy but he realized the deplorable state religiously
that the Boston Anglicans would be in if no minister of
their faith was left in the town. Accordingly, he went

to Mr. Parker and told him that as he, occupying a secondary position in Trinity Church, had not aroused the antagonism of the Patriots he would be safe in staying and that he had better not desert his people. M͞r Parker took his advice and stayed, with the result that in 1804 he became for a year (until his death) the second Bishop of Massachusetts. The evacuation took place in March, and the following July, on M͞r Parker's representing that he could no longer safely pray for the King, the wardens and vestry instructed him to omit the prayers for the Royal Family. — Foote's "History of King's Chapel," Vol. 2, pp. 306–309.

DOCTOR BYLES'S CHIEF PUBLISHED WRITINGS

A Poem on the Death of His late Majesty King George, of Glorious Memory, and the Accession of our Present Sovereign, King George II, to the British Throne. Printed in 1727.

A Poem presented to His Excellency William Burnet, Esq.; on his arrival at Boston, July 19, 1728. Printed in 1728.

The Character of the Perfect and Upright Man; his Peaceful End described; and Our Duty to observe it laid down. In a Discourse on Psalm 37 : 37. Printed for S. Gerrish, 1729.

A Discourse on the Present Vileness of the Body, and its Future Glorious Change by Christ. To which is added a Sermon on the Nature and Importance of Conversion. Both occasionally deliver'd at Dorchester April 23, 1732. Printed by S. Kneeland and T. Green for N. Proctor, 1732.

The Faithful Servant, Approv'd at Death, and Entring into the Joy of His Lord. A Sermon at the Publick Lecture in Boston, July 27, 1732. Occasioned by the much lamented Death of the Honourable Daniel Oliver, Esq.; one of His Majesty's Council for the Province. Who Deceased there the 23ᵈ of the same month, in the 69ᵗʰ year of His Age. . . . With a Poem by Mr. Byles. [Psalm 12 : 1.] Printed by S. Kneeland and T. Green for D. Henchman, in Cornhill, 1732. Second title, An Elegy, address'd to His Excellency Governour Belcher: on the Death of his Brother-in-law, the Honourable Daniel Oliver, Esq.

To His Excellency Governour Belcher, on the Death of His Lady. An Epistle. By the Reverend Mʳ Byles. Printed in 1736.

On the Death of the Queen. A Poem. Inscribed to His Excellency Governour Belcher. By the Reverend Mʳ Byles. Printed by J. Draper, for D. Henchman in Cornhill, 1738.

Affection on Things Above. A Discourse delivered at the Thursday Lecture in Boston, December 11, 1740. Printed in 1740, by G. Rogers and D. Fowle for J. Edwards and H. Foster, in Cornhill.

The Glories of the Lord of Hosts, and the Fortitude of the Religious Hero. A Sermon preached to the Ancient and Honourable Artillery Company, June 2, 1740. Being the Anniversary of their Election of Officers. [Text II Kings 9 : 4, 5, 6.] Printed in 1740, and sold by Thomas Fleet and Joseph Edwards at their shop in Cornhill. (Reprinted in *General Magazine and Historical Chronicle*, Vol. 1, pp. 34–35, Philadelphia, 1741.)

R

The Flourish of the Annual Spring, Improved in a Sermon Preached at the Ancient Thursday Lecture in Boston, May 3, 1739. [Text, Numbers 17 : 8.] Printed in 1741, and sold by Rogers and Fowle at the Printing Office over against the South-east Corner of the Town House.

Repentance and Faith the Great Doctrine of the Gospel of Universal Concernment. Printed in 1741, and sold by J. Eliot.

The Visit to Jesus by Night. In Evening Lecture. Printed by Rogers and Fowle, at the head of Queen Street, near the Town House, in 1741.

The Character of the Perfect and Upright Man, His Peaceful End Described; and our duty to observe it laid down, in a Discourse on Psalm 37 : 37. To which is added an Exemplification of the Subject in a Short Account of the Peaceful Death of Mrs Anna Byles. By Mr. Byles. The Second Edition. Printed by B. Green and Company for D. Gookin, at the corner of Water Street, Cornhill, 1744.

The Comet: A Poem. Printed and sold by B. Green and Company in Newbury Street, and D. Gookin at the corner of Water Street, Cornhill, 1744.

God Glorious in the Scenes of the Winter. A Sermon preach'd at Boston, December 23, 1744. Printed by B. Green and Company for D. Gookin, over against the Old South Meeting House, 1744.

Poems on Several Occasions. By Mr. Byles. Printed by S. Kneeland and T. Green, 1744. This collection includes thirty-two poems, several of which are given separately in the present list. One poem of this collection is addressed, "To the Rev. D.ʳ Watts on his Divine Poems." The preface to the collection says: "The Poems collected in these Pages were for the most Part written as the Amusements of looser Hours, while the Author belonged to the College, and was unbending his Mind from severer Studies, in the Entertainments of the Classicks. Most of them have been several Times printed here, at London, and elsewhere, either separately or in Miscellanies: And the Author has now drawn them into a Volume. Thus he gives up at once these lighter Productions, and bids adieu to the airy Muse."

The Glorious Rest of Heaven, A Sermon at the Thursday Lecture in Boston, January 3, 1744/5. By Mr. Byles. [Text, Matt. 17:4.] Published at the Request of many of the Hearers. Printed by B. Green and Company for D. Gookin, over against the Old South Meeting House, 1745.

The Prayer and Plea of David to be delivered from Blood-guiltiness, Improved in a Sermon at the Ancient Thursday Lecture in Boston, May 16ᵗʰ, 1751, Before the Execution of a Young Negro Servant for poisoning an Infant. [Psalm 40:9, 10.] Printed and sold by Samuel Kneeland, opposite the Prison in Queen Street, 1751.

God the Strength and Portion of His People under all the Exigencies of Life and Death: A Funeral Sermon on the Honourable Mʳˢ Katherine Dummer, the Lady of His Honour, William Dummer, Esq.; late Lieutenant Governor and Commander in Chief over this Province. Preach'd at Boston, January 9, 1752, the Lord's Day after her Death and Burial. Printed by John Draper, 1752.

Divine Power and Anger Displayed in Earthquakes.

A Sermon occasioned by the late Earthquake in New England, November 18, 1755. And Preached the next Lord's Day at Point Shirley. . . . Published at the Pressing Importunity of the Hearers. [Six lines of Scripture texts.] Printed and sold by S. Kneeland, in Queen Street, 1755.

The Conflagration, Applied to that Grand Period or Catastrophe of our World, when the face of Nature is to be changed by a Deluge of Fire, as formerly it was by that of Water. The God of Tempest and Earthquake. Printed and sold by D. Fowle, in Ann Street, and Z. Fowle, in Middle Street. The catalogue of the Boston Public Library gives the date as 1744, that of the Mass. Hist. Soc. as 1755. The poem was first printed in the *New-England Weekly Journal*, May 19, 1729.

The Man of God Thoroughly Furnished to Every Good Work. A Sermon preached at the ordination of the Reverend Mr. Mather Byles to the Pastoral Office, in the First Church of Christ in New London, November 18, 1757. To which is Added the Charge given him upon that Occasion. By his Father. [Text, Proverbs 23 : 15, 16.] Printed and sold by Nathaniel Green and Timothy Green, Jr., 1758. (The copy in the Mass. Hist. Soc. library has manuscript corrections by the author.)

The Vanity of Every Man at His Best Estate. A Funeral Sermon on the Honourable William Dummer, Esq., Late Lieutenant-Governor and Commander in Chief over the Province of the Massachusetts Bay in New England, who Died October 10, 1761. Aged 84 years. [Text, Ecclesiastes 12 : 7, 8.] Printed by Green and Russell in Boston, 1761.

The Flourish of the Annual Spring, Improved in a Sermon Preached at the Ancient Thursday Lecture in Boston, May 3, 1739. With a Hymn for the Spring. The Second Edition. Boston: Reprinted by Thomas and John Fleet at the Heart and Crown in Cornhill in 1769. (The copy in the Massachusetts Historical Society Library has in it the autograph "Catharine Byles.")

The Glories of the Lord of Hosts, and the Fortitude of the Religious Hero. A Sermon preached to the Ancient and Honourable Artillery Company, June 2, 1740. Being the Anniversary of their Election of Officers. [Text II Kings 9 : 4, 5, 6.] The Third Edition. Reprinted by Thomas and John Fleet, at the Heart and Crown in Cornhill, 1769.

A Sermon on the Nature and Necessity of Conversion, reprinted by Edes and Gill in 1769 [First printed in 1732].

New England Hymn [Adapted to tune America]. Printed in "The New England Psalm-Singer or American Chorister." Edes and Gill, probably 1770.

A Discourse on the Present Vileness of the Body and Its Future Glorious Change by Christ. [Text, Acts 17 : 18.] The Second Edition. Reprinted by Thomas and John Fleet, at the Heart and Crown, in Cornhill, 1771. Printed with this sermon, in the second edition, is an essay called "The Meditation of Cassim, the Son of Ahmed," which was first printed in the *New-England Weekly Journal* in 1727.

The Death of a Friend lamented and improved. A Funeral Sermon on John Gould, Esq.; who Died January 8, 1772. Boston: Printed by Richard Draper, 1772.

An "Epistle," in two pages, introducing a sermon on

the death of "the Honorable Abigail Belcher, late Consort of Jonathan Belcher, Esq.; Late Lieutenant Governor and Commander in Chief and His Majesty's present Chief Justice of His Province of Nova Scotia, delivered at Halifax in the said Province, October 20, 1771, by John Secombe of Chester, A.M. With an Epistle by Mather Byles, D.D., of Boston." [Texts, John 17:24; Luke 23:43.] Boston, New England, Printed by Thomas and John Fleet, 1772. The "Epistle" is addressed to Chief Justice Jonathan Belcher of Nova Scotia, son of Governor Jonathan Belcher, and is signed, "Your Honour's most affectionate Kinsman and faithful Friend and Servant, Mather Byles," and dated "Boston, January, 20, 1772." [Rev. John Secombe was a Congregational minister settled at Chester, Nova Scotia.]

DRAFTS OF LETTERS IN MANUSCRIPT

A list of the names of persons to whom drafts of letters in manuscript are found in D.ʳ Byles's letter book in the library of the New England Historic Genealogical Society is as follows:

M.ʳ Alexander Pope, Oct. 7, 1727.

The Honourable Isaac Winslow, Esq., Marshfield. No date.

The Rev. Mr. James Gardner, pastor of the Church in Marshfield. No date.

The Rev. Mr. Isaac Watts at my Lady Asbury's, in Lime-Street, London, May 3, 1728.

M.ʳ Alexander Pope, May 18, 1728.

Alexander Pope, Esq., Nov. 25, 1728.

The Reverend Isaac Watts, D.D., May 8, 1729.

M.ʳ Nathanael Walter in Glocester, Oct. 14, 1729.

The Right Honourable John Lord Barrington at Beckett House, Dec. 15, 1730.

The Right Honourable George Granville My Lord Lansdowne, Dec. 15, 1730.

The Right Honourable George, Lord Lansdowne, March 4, 173½.

The Reverend M.ʳ Thomas Bradbury, London, March 4, 173½.

The Rev. D.ʳ Isaac Watts, Jan. 3, 1736/7.

Alexander Pope, Esqr., Twickenham. No date.

M.ʳ James Thomson. To be left in New-Street, London, Jan. 4, 1736/7.

The Honourable D.ʳ Benjamin Franklin, London. No date.

The Rev.ᵈ D.ʳ John Chalmers, Principal of the King's College and University of Aberdeen. No date.

His Excellency the Governor [Hutchinson], April 3, 1771.

The Honourable Andrew Oliver, Esq.ʳ, Salem. No date.

M.ʳˢ Livingstone, sent the Day after her Husband and others had been here on a visit, when 300 dollars was found left in the chamber closet. May 24, 1780.

M.ʳ Murray, Glocester, Jan., 1781.

M.ʳ Enoch Brown, Boston, Feb. 10, 1781.

His daughter-in-law in Halifax, on the death of his [second] wife. No date.

M.ʳ Frederick William Geyer, London, July 1, 1783.

M.ʳ Holmes, London, Nov. 4, 1783.

M.ʳ Frederick William Geyer, merchant in London, Nov. 14, 1783.

His daughter-in-law in Halifax, Dec. 10, 1784.

Rev. Ezra Stiles, President of Yale College, New Haven, April 13, 1787.

D.̇ Byles, Halifax, April 14, 1787.

His Excellency Benjamin Franklin, Esq.̇, Philadelphia, May 14, 1787.

M.̇ Gawen Brown, Petersburg, Virginia, May 14, 1787.

[Following these letters of D.̇ Byles's are many from his daughters to various friends, especially their brother and his family in Halifax.]

INDEX

Adams, Elizabeth (Hill), 239.
Adams, Rev. John, 98.
Adams, Joseph, 239.
Adams, Samuel, 147, 239.
Almon, Dr. William Bruce, 12.
Almon, family, of Halifax, Nova Scotia, 238.
Amory, John, 52.
Amory, Mrs. John, 52.
Appleton, Rev. Nathaniel, 232.
Apthorp, Mrs. John, 52.
Artillery Company, 84.
Attucks, Crispus, 146.
Auchmuty, Judge Robert, Jr., 184.

Bailey, Rev. Jacob, 167–169, 235.
Barrett, Mrs. John, 53.
Bass, Alden, 231.
Belcher, Andrew, 38, 39, 60.
Belcher, Andrew, Jr., 45, 46.
Belcher, Ann, 42.
Belcher, family, 41, 60, 61, 246.
Belcher, Governor Jonathan, 38, 39, 43, 58, 130, 179, 226, 229.
Belcher, Mrs. Jonathan, 58–60.
" Belcher Papers," 226.
Belcher, Sarah, 46.
Belknap, Rev. Jeremy, 88, 119, 126, 158, 169, 198–200, 203, 228, 233, 235, 236.
" Belknap Papers," 228, 234, 237.
Belknap, Sarah (Byles), 198.

Bennett, Joseph's account of Boston, 48–51.
Billings, William, 110.
Blake, John, 231.
Blood, Henry Ames, 232.
Bolton, Charles Knowles, 237.
Bolton, church at, 159.
Board of War, warrant to deliver Byles to, 165.
Boston, Athenæum, 184; beacon, 181; Beacon Hill, 181; Common, 181, 182; Copp's Hill, 13; Dock Square, 13; evacuation of, by General Howe, 174, 240; *Evening Post*, 237; *Gazette*, 27, 34, 226, 235; Mall, 49, 50, 217; mansions, 182–185; ministers, doggerel ballad on, 120; *News-Letter*, 235; North Square, 14; Old North or Second Church, 14; in Provincial period, 180–185; "Pulpit of the Revolution," 143; in the seventeenth century, 13, 14; siege of, 143; social history of, in the Provincial period, 47; Tileston Street, 16; Town House, 181; wharves, 181.
Bowdoin, James, 184.
" Bower of Taste," 236.
Bowman, Rev. Jonathan, 37.
Boylston, Elizabeth, 68.

political sympathies, 143–146; aristocratic tendencies and social position, 5, 86, 178–180; prejudices against him, 5, 6, 88; a friend of British officers and staunch Tory in the Revolution, 2, 3, 4, 6, 148, 150, 151, 155, 156; watches funeral procession of Crispus Attucks, 146; trial before his church, 9, 154–157, 171, 172; disapproval of other ministers of the course of the church, 157–159; tried before the town and sentenced to transportation, but sentence not carried out, 6, 7, 89, 161–167; imprisoned in his house, 166, 167; his daughter Catherine's account of the two trials, 170–172; life after the Revolution, 88, 89, 196; friendship with Rev. Nathaniel Emmons, 90, 91; relations with Dr. Benjamin Franklin, 185–195; probably attended Trinity Church, 201; visited by Rev. Jacob Bailey, 167; is seized with paralysis, 198; Dr. Belknap describes his infirmities, 199; taken from his house in the great fire, 200, 201; tender relations with his son, 212; visit of Rev. Samuel Parker to him when he was dying, 202; his death, 202, 203; buried in the Granary burying-ground, 203; money subscribed for his funeral expenses, 237; theological position, 78; made no

original contribution to theology, 75; a brilliant preacher, 5, 79; his printed sermons, 78, 79; avoids politics in the pulpit, 143–145; prays at town meeting and preaches Thursday Lectures, 84, 106; "lashed" by Rev. Eleazer Wheelock, 87; Rev. John Eliot's criticism, 73; Rev. John Eliot's account of (in 1777), 158; Ephraim Eliot's strictures on, 159; showed no desire to become an Anglican, 84; character of his ministry, 75; presence, voice, dress, 9–11; portraits of, 10–12; prolific writings, 2; attempt of friends to exalt as a great poet, 98–100; a "New England poet laureate," 178; Epistles to Governor Belcher, 61–65, 98; poem of welcome to Governor Burnet, 95, 96; "The Conflagration," written in his fifteenth year, 96–98; letter to Pope, 101–103; correspondence with Pope, Watts, and Grenville, 103, 104, 105, 233; poem to Dr. Watts, 112–114; receives the Odyssey from Pope and inscribes lines in it, 105, 106; attention to the art of poetry, 106–108; interest in music, 111; interest in natural science, 91; his overflowing wit, 1, 2, 4; Lucius Manlius Sargent characterizes his humour, 233; pun on the names Quincy and Byles, 55; pas-